MAHMOUD NAKUA — LIBYA. Tripoli

news EDITOR. Libyan BROADCASTING

dec 1967

News
Broadcasting
Tripoli, Libya

ISLAM
THE MISUNDERSTOOD
RELIGION

BY

MUHAMMAD QUTB

PUBLISHED BY

MINISTRY OF AWQAF & ISLAMIC AFFAIRS

STATE OF KUWAIT

An English translation of the sixth edition of the Arabic

Text published in Cairo 1964.

Printed By : Al-Assriya Printing Press — Kuwait

بِسْمِ اللهِ الرَّحْمٰنِ الرَّحِيمِ

فَأَمَّا ٱلَّذِينَ فِي قُلُوبِهِمْ زَيْغٌ فَيَتَّبِعُونَ مَا تَشَابَهَ مِنْهُ
ٱبْتِغَاءَ ٱلْفِتْنَةِ وَٱبْتِغَاءَ تَأْوِيلِهِ

(آل عمران ٧)

" In the name of Allah, Most Gracious, Most Merciful "

".....But those in whose hearts is perversity follow the part thereof that is allegorical, seeking discord, and searching for its hidden meanings"

The Holy Quran 3 : 7

— 3 —

FOREWARD

The Ministry of Awqaf and Islamic Affairs has the pleasure to introduce this book to the English speaking readers. By doing so the Ministry tries to carry out the recommendation made by the members of the National Assembly to lay great stress on the preaching of Islam throughout the world and in the continent of Africa in particular. This is also in line with the government policy as expressed in the Amiri Speech.

The merit of this book is that it dispels the doubts cast against Islam by its enemies. It successfully attempts to prove to the young generation of Muslims and to the whole world at large, that Islam is not only a living force but also the only means of salvation for the complex maladies and problems of the twentieth century.

By supervising the translation of this book from Arabic the Department of Islamic Affairs hopes to achieve the desired objective. While wishing to express its gratitude to all those who helped in the preparation of this book, the Department begs to be excused for any shortcomings which are expected of this first attempt.

Kuwait

January, 1967

**Dept. of Islamic Affairs,
Ministry of Awqaf &
Islamic Affairs.**

CONTENTS

		Page
1.	Preface	7
2.	Is Religion Antiquated ?	19
3.	Islam and Slavery	62
4.	Islam and Feudalism	112
5.	Islam and Capitalism	132
6.	Islam and Private Ownership	144
7.	Islam and Class System	158
8.	Islam and Alms	165
9.	Islam and Woman	173
10.	Islam and the Concept of Punishment	244
11.	Islam and Civilization	255
12.	Islam and Reactionarism	261
13.	Islam and Sexual Repression	274
14.	Islam and Freedom of Thought	284
15.	Religion : the Opium of the People	293
16.	Islam and Non-Muslim Communities	309
17.	Islam and Idealism	318
18.	Islam and Communism	333
19.	What Next?	352

PREFACE TO THE SIXTH EDITION

As I wrote this book over the years I did not entertain the hope that it would elicit such a warm reception and appreciation. And when it went to the press over and over again I thanked God and felt grateful to the readers who took so much interest in the contents of this book.

I was however beginning to feel that in the future this book need not be republished. For, in my view, we had better now say something positive about Islam itself in the context of the various fields of life it embraces, and the positivity and the supervisory character that its law enjoys with regard to practical life, as I have attempted in the books appearing after the present one, instead of limiting our efforts to defending it against the various doubts given currency to by its enemies in order to confuse and throw us on the defensive.

But when I read the orientalist Mr. Wilfred Cantwill Smith's book " Islam in Modern History", and found that the author had in three places referred to this book of mine in words so angry and disparaging that came very near to openly calling

— 7 —

names, I decided that the book that had roused the anger of a rancorous crusader to such an extent must remain in circulation and be published over and over again.

All my thanks are due to Allah ; His Grace alone brings succour.

MUHAMMAD QUTB

PREFACE

The Majority of the modern" educated " people are today faced with a religious crisis. Is religion really a fact of life ? It might have been one in the past, but does it still remain so in the world of today when science has changed the whole course of life, and when there is no place in it for anything save science and what scientific facts approve of ? Does religion represent a genuine need of humanity ? Or is it something wholly dependent upon the temperamental constitution of an individual ? so that one may or may not believe in it as there is no difference between the two states, of belief and unbelief ?

Talking about Islam they betray a similar state of intellectual crisis when the missionaries of Islam tell them that Islam is not a mere creed, nor does it represent simply an edification of souls, or a refinement and training of human virtues but is rather a harmonious whole that also includes a just economic system, a well balanced social organization, codes of civil, criminal as well as international law, a philosophical outlook upon life along with a system of physical instruction, all of them flowing from the same fundamental creed of Islam and its moral and spiritual temperament. When they hear all this, these " educated " people are greatly perplexed, for they supposed that Islam had since long ceased to exist as it had become outmoded and had exhausted all its usefulness. That is why they are surprised when they hear devout Muslims saying that Islam does not belong to a remote past, it is not obsolete or antiquated but is a living and flourishing system of life even at the present moment, as it holds within itself such elements of life as no other system known to humanity does, including socialism as well as communism or any other system.

At this their surprise exceeds limits, they can no more contain themselves, so they scream at these preachers of God's word : Do you tell us all this about the religion that approves of slavery, feudalism and captialism — the system which holds that woman is only a half-man and imprisons her within her household ; which prescribes such punishments as stoning to death, mutilation and whipping ; which lets its people live on charity ; which splits them up into different classes, some exploiting the others ; a system which provides no security of a decent living to the toiling people ; and a system which is such and such, how is it possible that such a system should even hold its own today, let alone its survival in the future ? Not to speak of its triumph and contending successfully, how can such a system even hold out in the ruthless ideological struggle going on at present among different modern socio-economic systems ?

Before proceeding further let us however pause a while and see as to who these "educated" skeptics are ? Whence does their skepticism originate ? Is this attitude of mind a result of their own free thinking or are they merely parroting the words of others without even so much as understanding them ?

The fact is that the skepticism exhibited by these gentlemen is not at all a result of their own independent thinking, nor did it originate in their own minds as such. For its true source we will have to go back a little over the history of modern times.

The middle ages witnessed crusades between Europe and the world of Islam. Furious battles were fought between the two after which followed a period that saw a suspension of hostilities between the two camps but their hostility towards each other never ended as is well borne out by what Lord Allenby said in clear terms on the occasion of the British occupation of Jerusalem in the First World War : " Now have the crusades come to an end ! ! "

We must also keep in mind that during the last two centuries European imperialism remained in conflict with the Islamic Orient. The British stepped into Egypt in 1882 following Taufiq's treachery. They hatched a plot with him for the military occupation of Egypt in order to thwart the popular revolution under the leadership of Orabi. Thereafter the British policy of necessity revolved around one basic aim : strengthening their hold more and more on the Islamic world and safeguarding their interests from being swept away by the true Islamic spirit of the Orient. We would in this respect like to refer to what the British prime minister of the Victorian age, Mr. Gladstone said in the House of Commons. Holding up the Holy Quran in his hands he told members of the House : " So long as the Egyptians have got this book with them, we will never be able to enjoy quiet or peace in that land."

Naturally the policy pursued by the British was one of deriding Islamic laws and principles, of exiling the sense of their sanctity from Muslims' hearts, and of painting Islam in the blackest of colours so as to make them look down upon it and in due course of time to discard it totally. They did all this in order to tighten up their imperialistic grip on this country.

The educational policy they adopted in Egypt was such as left the students quite ignorant about the reality of Islam, except that it was a religion embracing worships, prayers, praising and glorifying God, and pursuing mystic practices; that the Quran was a book read in order to invoke God's blessings and that Islam was a theoretical invitation to pursue the noblest and most generous of moral precepts. Students were never told anything about Islam as a socio-economic system of government or as a constitution, or as a basis of internal and external policy, or as a system of education, or as a way of life and a watcher over life. What they were taught instead was the doubts cast against Islam by the orientalists and other European crusaders in order to make the Muslims forsake their religion and succumb easily to the evil machinations of imperialism.

They were taught that the only genuine social system in existence was that which Europe possessed, the only true economic system was one that was conceived by the European philosophers : the right and most appropriate form of constitutional govern-ment was what the Europeans, thanks to their various experiments, evolved. They were taught that the rights of man were first taken cognizance of by the French revolution ; that democracy was fostered and made popular by the English people ; and that it was the Roman Empire that provided any basis of civilization. In short the British depicted Europe as a rebellious but mighty giant with none to stand in its way or check its progress whereas they presented the East as a dwarfish underling with no standing of its own save that of subordination to Europe and complete dependence upon it for its social and cultural outlook.

This political policy at last took effect. Among the Egyptians there sprang up generations who were shorn of any thoughts of their individuality or independent cultural existence. They were completely enthralled by Europe ; they worshipped it most devotedly ; they could neither see with their own eyes nor were they any more left capable of thinking for themselves; they would see just what the Europeans wanted them ; and they thought what they wished them to think.

The " educated " intelligentsia of today represents as such the culminating point of what the imperialists with their political manoeuvres achieved in this country.

These poor people know nothing about Islam but doubts. About Islam they have no information save what they received through their European masters. That is why they are seen shouting like them advocating the separation of religion from the state and of science from Islam.

But in their ignorance they pass by the fact that the religion that Europe shook off was one quite different from what the advocates of Islamic ideology call upon people to adopt ; and that the particular circumstances that prevailed in Europe at the time and made it turn its back upon religion were confined to that region of the world only. Nothing of the sort ever happened in the Islamic Orient ; nor is there any likelihood of its ever happening there. Thus when they call upon their countrymen to discard Islam or declare that Islam should have no say in the management of social, political and economic affairs of the community and life, they are merely expressing and parroting the imported thoughts of their masters.

Europe was the scene of a conflict between religion and science, because the church there had arbitrarily embraced certain theories and dogmas (inheriting them from Greece) and insisted that they were sacred and a gospel truth. So when the theoretical and the empirical science demonstrated the error and fallacy of these theories, the people there had no other course but to believe in science and disbelieve in the church as well as in the religion these churchmen stood for. The war between religion and science gained in intensity and the enthusiasm to get free from the dominance of these religious men increased as the church in Europe conferred upon itself divine power and proceeded to enforce it in a most tyrannical manner. Thus for the people there religion came to signify an abominable ghoul that harassed them in their working no less than in their sleeping hours. It exacted from men costly extortions and reduced them to an abject state of subordination to the churchmen, besides calling upon them to swallow nonsense and superstitions in the name of God. The torturing of scientists and burning them alive because they said, for instance, that the earth was round, was the ugliest of crimes that made it a sacred duty of every sensible, free-thinking and conscientious individual there to come forward and help the forces that sought to destroy this abnominable ghoul or at least put it in chains so as not to let it ever again harass and oppress the people besides harming the cause of religion by misrepresenting it and making others feel as if religion contained nothing but falsehood and untruth.

But what about us, we who live in the Islamic East ? Why should we separate science from religion or hold that the two are at variance and war with each other ? Is there even a single scientific fact which has been found to contradict Islam and its basic creed ? Were scientists ever subjected to persecution in the domain of Islam ? The whole history of Islam is before us. It testifies that there have been great doctors, astronomers, mathematicians, physicists as well as chemists but never were they persecuted for their views. There is no trace of any conflict between science and their religious beliefs to be found in the minds of these great Muslim scientists. Nor did there exist any hostilities between them and the ruling authorities such as might have led to their suffering or burning alive.

What is it then that makes these " educated " people plead for separation of religion from science, for attacking Islam and finding faults with it without any understanding or knowledge of it ? Their feverish crying is nothing but a symptom of the poison that had been administered to them by the imperialists, of course, without their knowing it.

This class of the " educated " elite was not at all in my mind when I wrote this book. They would never return to what is right until their masters in the West also do turn towards it after despairing of their Godless materialistic civilization and recognize that it can bring them no salvation, and so return to a system of life that is at once spiritual as well as practical a system embracing belief no less than life at once and at the same time.

I had rather another class before me in writing this book — the sincere and enlightened youth, who earnestly wish to find out the reality, the truth, but the doubts and lies spread about Islam by the deceitful imperialistic powers leave them helpless to see the light, or the answer to these lies, and so they are left groping about in darkness, for the slaves of imperialism and the devils of communism would not let them march out to the right path — the path to freedom, honour and sublimity. It is to this enlightened and sincere group of young men that I present this book and hope that it may please God to help me dispel doubts about Islam from their minds.

IS RELIGION ANTIQUATED ?

Dazzled by the achievements of science during the 18th and 19th centuries many westerners thought that religion had exhausted all its usefulness and surrendered to science once for all. Almost all the eminent western psychologists and sociologists expressed themselves in similar terms. Thus Freud, the renowned psychologist, for instance, showing the futility of any advocacy for what religion stood for in modern time says that the human life passes through three distinct psychological phases : superstition, religion and science. Now being the era of science all religion was out of date.

As we have already explained in the preface there were certain causes which led the men of science in Europe to adopt a view of life antagonistic to religion, and based on its hatred. It was due to the great controversy, that raged there between men of science and the Christian church, which made them think — quite justifiably of course — that whatever the church stood for was reactionary, retrogressive, backward and superstitious, and that therefore it must of necessity vacate its seat for science so as to enable humanity to move ahead on the path of civilization.

Without appreciating the difference between the peculiar conditions of life obtaining in Europe at the time of this unhappy conflict and those in their own Islamic orient, people opposed to their sacred traditions handed down to them from past generations demanded their outright abolition. Then came the contagion of imitation which plagued the dominated Islamic Orient and led the naive among its people to fancy that the only way to progress was that followed by the dominant nations of Europe, and that they have to discard their religion just as Europe had already done failing which they feared that they would be trapped in an abyss of re-actionarism, backwardness and humbug.

But such people overlooked the fact that even in the West, not all the outstanding scholars were antagonistic towards religion ; nor do their works exhibit anything of this sort. On the other hand we find some intellectuals among them of great emin-ence, who, freed of the materialism of the Godless Europe, were driven to the conclusion that religion is a psychological as well as an intellectual necessity for mankind.

The most noted figure among them is the astronomer James Jeans who started his intellectual career as a Godless sceptic but was led finally by his scientific explorations to the conclusion that the greatest problems of science could not be resolved without believing in God. The famous sociologist Jeans Bridge went so far as to eulogize Islam for achieving a successful amalgam of the temporal with the spiritual into a harmonious system of thought blent with a practical code of life. The well-known English writer Somerset Maugham epitomized the whole attitude of modern Europe towards religion when he remarked that Europe had in the present era discovered a new God — science, discarding the older one.

The God of Science has however turned out to be extremely fickle, everchanging and constantly shifting positions, upholding today as a fact and reality what it rejected yesterday as false and spurious and vice versa, with the result that we see its " worshippers " doomed to a fate of perpetual restlessness and anxiety, for how can they find rest and peace of mind under such a capricious God ? That this constant restlessness with which the modern west is afflicted is a fact, is borne out by the large number of psychological and nervous disorders that are so common in the western community of today.

A still another result of this deification of modern science is that the world we live in, is devoid of all meaning and purpose with no higher order or power to guide it, with a persistent struggle is ever going on between opposing forces. As a result everything in this world suffers change : economic and political systems change ; relations between states and individuals alter ; even scientific " Facts " do change. What can man expect save misery and perpetual restlessness in a world with such a sombre setting where no Higher Power exists whom he should turn to for support, strength and comfort in this ruthless struggle of life.

It is religion and religion alone that can restore to the world of humanity peace and tranquility. It instils in man love for goodness and courage to stand up to the forces of evil and tyranny as a necessary condition of obtaining God's pleasure and to make His will predominant on this earth awaiting with patience for his reward in the Hereafter. Doesn't mankind really need peace, tranquility, comfort, in a word, religion ?

What will become of man but for faith and belief in an eternal life in the hereafter? In this context man's life upon earth assumes new dimensions opening far higher horizons of progress before him, in the absence of which he is inevitably oppressed by a torturous sense of nothingness, as it means a virtual cutting short of man's total life-span, making him a mere plaything in the hands of his whims and caprices which teach him nothing but to derive the maximum possible amount of pleasure during this short sojourn upon earth. Mutual rivalries, savage battles and conflicts over the possession of material gains follow, as now there is no Higher Power to lay checks on men's desires. So, blinded by their greed and lust, each one of them wants to gain whatever he can lay his hands on in the shortest possible time.

Thus man is degraded to lower planes of feelings and thought. His imagination sinks low and so do his ideals and the means to achieve them. They are all marked with abjectness. Mankind is doomed to a perpetual life of hideous internecine wars that scarcely permit it to soar to higher and nobler ends in life. In such a world there is no room for love or sympathy, as men are wholly obsessed with their carnal pleasures. They are led by their blind passions. How can they in such a context have lofty aspirations or even appreciate genuine human feelings ?

Men in such a world no doubt gain some material profits. But of what use are these when fellowmen are constantly wrangling over them, each ready to cut his brother's throat should he find it opportune for his own material welfare ? Materialism spoils life so much that even man's material achievements are rendered useless and senseless. Men are enslaved by greed, lust and avarice. Blind appetites alone govern them. They have no control whatsoever over them. Nor can they ever hope to extricate themselves from their trammels.

Similarly the nations too, due to similar causes, get entangled in devastating wars which spoil all harmony in life. And science with all its dreadful weapons, is employed for the extermination of the human-race and its obliteration rather than make it serve man and contribute towards his well-being.

Viewed in this context religion means broadening the mental horizon of mankind, for life is not confined to this world alone but continues even beyond it — up to an eternity. This brightens hope in man's

heart and encourages him to fight stead-
fastly against evil and oppression. Religion
teaches love, sympathy and universal brotherhood
and is thus the only way to peace, prosperity and
progress which is in itself a sufficient reason for its
retention. It equips man in the best possible way
for the hard struggle of life.

Furthermore it is faith and faith alone that can
inspire man to rise above his self and suffer
for the noble and lofty ideals. Once taken
away from him he is left with nothing else to
look up or pin his hopes to outside his own self. He
changes into a brute immediately. Many a man fell
fighting in the noble cause of truth spending the
whole of their lives in the struggle yet achieving
nothing in the materialistic sense of the word. What
inspired these noble souls to engage in a battle that
brought them no material rewards, that caused them
rather lose whatever little they happened to possess?
Undoubtedly it was one of the many miracles of
the Faith, for, so far as selfish motives viz. avarice,
greed, lust etc, are concerned these can never make
man achieve anything really good, noble or of a
permanent value. This is why the material triumphs
won by selfish avarice are so short-lived and temporary
as the incentive for immediate gain cannot equip

man with the character, nor can it give him the courage to stand fast suffering patiently and for long for a truly noble and lofty cause.

There are in fact some so-called " reformers" who seek inspiration from hatred rather than love. This is the headspring of their inspiration, which they say gives them the courage to bear hardships for their cause with patience. The hatred they cherish may be personal in character or it may spring among a class of people and be directed against mankind in general or the generation they may have happened to be born in. Such rancour-inspired people may realize some of their ends by way of " reformation." Their rancour coupled with their fiery and innate cruel natures may as well sustain them and boost their " morale " to willingly suffer privations for the sake of the cause they stand for, but a doctrine based on malevolence rather than love can never lead humanity to anything good. They may remove certain evils and put an end to the existing state of injustice but offer no sound remedy for these ailments of mankind. Based on hatred and malevolence, such a philosophy of life is bound sooner or later to degenerate and create far more evil and injustice than that it had originally professed and sought to cure.

On the other hand a creed that does not aim at the immediate gains of this world, nor derives inspiration from malevolence but fosters in men noble passions of love, fraternity and a will to lay down their lives serving their fellowmen can alone guarantee to humanity a reward permanent and worth striving for, and pave the way to its future progress and prosperity. The essence of such a creed is faith in God and His love with a consequent virtuous mode of living that helps man get nearer unto his Creator. But both of these remain lifeless so long as one does not believe in the Hereafter as well. Belief in the Hereafter gives man a sense of security banishing from his heart fear of extinction with his physical death and promising him an eternal life. This in other words means that his efforts shall not be wasted away but shall be crowned with their fullest reward in the life to come, if not in the life herein.

All this is however what follows as a natural corollary to a simple belief in God and the Hereafter as such. But so far as Islam is concerned it does not stop short there, but goes a long way ahead: it has a quite different and far more fascinating story to tell.

Those who may imagine that Islam has become outmoded and is no longer needed, do not know as to what it stands for, nor do they in any wise seem to understand its real mission in human life. As taught to them in the history books prescribed by the agents of imperialism in early life they think that Islam was revealed merely to put an end to idolatry and guide man to the worship of God alone , that the Arabs were torn into antagonistic tribes, Islam came and united them and made them a strong and unified nation , that they were addicted to drinking and gambling and led depraved lives, so Islam came and checked them from these depravities as it did abolish so many other evil customs prevalent among them such as burying alive their daughters and wasting away their strength in acts of revenge ; and that Islam called upon Muslims to disseminate its message which they did, this in turn leading to the battles that ultimately determined the boundaries of the Islamic world as we know it today. This was then according to these people the sole purpose of Islam in human-life !! "It being a historical mission has long since been fulfilled : there is no idol-worship in the Islamic world ; the once antagonistic tribes have been more or less subject to a process of absorption losing their identity in the larger nationalities or communities. As far as gambling and drinking are concerned let us bear in mind that human civilization has advanced to such an extent now that it is useless to declare such pastimes unlawful as we see that despite all religious taboos they still persist. It is no use insisting on their abolition. Thus they conclude that Islam has served its purpose in this world ; it has had its day but is now quite out of place and is therefore no longer needed. We must, therefore, turn towards the modern doctrines of life as in these alone lies our salvation."

Thus parroting the ideas of their western teachers these people betray their own ignorance. They know nothing about Islam or its real mission in human life. Let us therefore, before proceeding further, see what Islam is, and what in fact it stands for ?

Islam, in a word, means liberation from all sorts of slavery such as may inhibit the progress of humanity or may not allow it to follow the path of virtue and goodness. It means man's freedom from dictators who enslave him by force or fear, make him do what is wrong and deprive him of his dignity, honour, property or even life. Islam liberates man from such tyranny by telling him that all authority vests in God and God alone ; He alone is the Real Sovereign. All men are His born subjects and as such He alone controls their destinies, none of them having the power to benefit aught or even avert any distress from his ownself contrary to or independent of His Divine Will. All men shall be presented before Him on the Day of Judgement to account for their performance in this life. Thus Islam brings to man freedom from fear or oppression inflicted on him by men like himself who are in reality as helpless as he, and who are no less subject to the Dominant will of God Almighty than he himself is.

Not only this but Islam means freedom from lust as well, including even the lust for life, as it is this very weakness of man which is exploited by tyrants and dictators intentionally or otherwise in enslaving their fellowmen. But for it no man would silently accept slavery to men like himself or sit idle to watch tyranny strut abroad and dare not challenge it. It is a great blessing of Islam that it taught man to fight tyranny and oppression bravely rather than cringe before them in abject servitude. Says the Holy Quran : " *Say* : *If it be that your fathers your sons, your brothers, your mates, or your kindred , the wealth that ye have gained , the commerce in which ye fear a decline , or the dwellings in which ye delight — are dearer to you than God, or His Apostle, or the striving in His cause , — then wait until God brings about His Decision : and God guides not the rebellious* " (9 : 24)

Contrasting the blind passions and appetites with the love of God, that represents in life love, virtue and truth and striving hard in His way — in the way of all that is good and lofty in life, Islam subjects the former to the latter. Unruly passions must be kept in check by the love of God ; it must be the dominant and real directing force in man's life as without this no man can claim to be a true Muslim

A man engrossed in sensual pleasures may form a mistaken outlook upon life and think that he enjoys life more than others do. But soon he realises his mistake as not long after this he is reduced to a mere slave to his blind passions. He is doomed to a perpetual life of deprivation and restlessness, for animal desires once run rampant are never satisfied : they are rather sharpened all the more and degrade man to lower levels of animalism where all his efforts are focussed on one object : how to derive the maximum possible sensual pleasure in life ? Such an attitude towards life is, however, not conducive to progress, material or spiritual, as humanity cannot soar in higher realms unless it is freed from the dominance of the blind animal appetites. Only then can it march ahead freely in the fields of science, arts or religion.

It is for this very reason that Islam attaches so great an importance to the freeing of man from his animal passions. For this purpose it neither favours monachism, nor does it forbid its followers to partake freely of the good things of this life. Rather it aims at the attainment of a balance between these two extremes. Whatever is here, is for man. They are to serve him, not to dominate or rule over him. He should not therefore allow himself to be made slave to these, should rather use them as means to a higher end *i.e.* his spiritual perfection by disseminating the word of God amongst his fellowmen. Thus Islam has a twofold objective in this regard : in the individual life it aims at making a just and sufficient provision to each and every individual so as to enable him to lead a decent, clean life ; and in the collective sphere it arranges things in such a way that all the social forces of a community are directed towards the enhancement of progress, and civilization in accordance with its basic outlook upon life that aims at striking a balance between the units and the whole, between individuals and the community.

Islam has also had the most liberalising effect on human intellect as it is diametrically opposed to all sorts of superstition Humanity has been in the course of history found to fall a prey to divers absurdities of thought as well as practice, some of which were the lively play of man's fancy and were acknowledged as such, whereas others were referred to as originating with Gods to whom human hands gave shape. Thus did the human intellect grope about in the dark before the advent of Islam. With Islam it attained maturity and freedom from this hotch-potch of nonsense, symbolised in these so-called gods, the Jewish traditions, and the imbecilities of the Christian Church, and was once again brought back to the folds of True Faith and True God.

Islam uses a very simple terminology. Its teachings are very easy to understand, perceive and believe in. It invites man to make use of the faculties given to him and try to acquire the fullest possible under-standing of life surrounding him. It does not as such admit of any inborn hostility between reason and religion or for that matter between science and re-ligion. It does not force man to believe in silly stuff as a prior condition to his belief in God. Nor does it compel him to renounce his God so as to be able to admit of scientific facts. Not content with this, Islam impresses upon man in clear and unequivocal terms that it is God and God alone who has in His immense mercy subjected all the things on this earth to man, and that all the facts that are discovered by scientific exploration or the material benefits that flow therefrom to man, are in fact a blessing of God, for which man should offer his thanks to God, and strive hard so as to become a worthy slave of so Merciful and Beneficent a Master. Thus Islam holds knowledge and science as a part of faith rather than regard them as an evil intrinsically opposed to genuine belief in God.

None of the above mentioned problems staring mankind in the face have yet been resolved ; the higher real human objectives are yet to be realized. Mankind is still the victim of various imbecilities, still groans under tyrants and dictators and is yet far from being free from the oppressive demands of animalism and of sensual pleasures. Islam has still a great and glorious part to play.

One half of the inhabitants of the world of today remain idol-worshippers as ever. As an instance we may refer to India, China and a great many other parts of the world that are inhabited by such people. The remaining half or thereabout dotes on still another type of deity that has exercised as great, nay a far worse corrupting influence on men's thoughts and feelings carrying them still further away from the right path. It is this very deity that is styled Modern Science.

Science is a powerful instrument to help us increase our knowledge of the things around us.

As such it has an impressive record of achievements to its credit. All these brilliant achievements were however, vitiated by one fatal mistake of the westerners : they installed science as supreme God declaring that it alone had the right to claim the adoration and submission of man unto it. Thus they denied themselves all means of acquiring knowledge save that recognized by empirical science which let humanity wander further away rather than bring it nearer to its real objective or destination. Consequently the otherwise vastly immense range of human endeavour and progress was shrunk small with the limitations such as all empirical sciences entail. For, in cases it is just possible that the scope of empirical science concerned as it is with mere matter may be narrower as against the inherent capacities of man or it may not be able to soar higher than man is otherwise capable of with wings not of intellect alone but with those lent him by his spirit as well, bringing him nearer to his Creator and enabling him at the same time to obtain a far sounder and more correct understanding of the ultimate reality.

The protagonists of science also claim that science alone can introduce man to the secrets of this universe and life ; hence, only that which is upheld by science is true ; the rest is all trash ! But while making such a statement they overlook the fact that science with all its brilliant and impressive record is still in its infancy and ever hesitant to commit itself as regards the veracity or supposititiousness of many things, for the simple reason that it cannot penetrate deep into the heart of reality beyond effecting a mere superfluous survey of it. But still its votaries clamour and tell us with a very authoritative air that there is no such thing as human soul in existence. They deny that man, confined as he is within the limitations of his sensory organs, can ever have any contact with the Unknown — not even a glimpse of it through telepathy[1] or dreams. They repudiate all these not because they have proved them to be mere illusions but simply because the experimental science with its inadequate instruments has not yet been able to fathom their mystery, as it pleased God to reserve these as something above and beyond the field of human perception. That it belongs in a higher order of things not subject to man's observation was however sufficient to make these gentlemen turn their backs

[1] Telepathy is the name for the communication of one mind with another at a distance. The most notable example of it is that incident wherein Caliph Omar called out to Sariah, a Muslim commander saying : " Sariah ! To the Mountain ! To the mountain ! " Sariah heard this warning coming from hundreds of miles away. So he led his contingent to the mountain, escaped the enemy lying in ambush and won a victory over them. As such telepathy though recognized as a scientific fact yet the modern scientist is so biased that its having anything to do with " soul " is denied outright. It is explained as a manifestation of a sixth but yet not fully explained faculty of the human-mind.

on it, some of them hurrying forward to announce to the awaiting world that there was no such thing as human soul in existence.

Such then is the " enlightened ignorance " man suffers from today, which shows how desperately he stands in need of Islam to blow away these " scientific " cobwebs of today as well as the imbecilities inherited from a remote past. Idol-worship was the older form wherein human folly found expression ; the cult of science-worship is its latest version. To liberate human reason and spirit, both of these needs must be shaken off. It is in this perspective that Islam emerges as the only hope for humanity, for it alone can restore peace between religion and science, bring back once more the tranquility and concord to this distressed world of today that has lost them through the perverted attitude towards life of the dominant West, forestalling an irreconcilable antagonism between man's reason and intuition, between his desire for knowledge and a craving for God.

Historically the modern European civilization is the descendent of the ancient Grecian civilization bequeathed to modern Europe by the Roman Empire. In this Grecian civilization the relations of man to his gods were viewed as of mutual antagonism and active antipathy. Thus the mysteries that human endeavour lays bare or the good things that he happens to lay his hands on in this world were viewed as something he forcibly wrenches from these jealous but ineffectual gods, who would ban and take back all these if they could. Viewed in this light the scientific achievements of man were just another name for his conquests that he won against his gods with a vengeance as they did not allow these willingly but only grudgingly.

It is this very pernicious spirit of the Grecian culture that still pervades the sub-conscious of the modern West. It is manifest sometimes in its interpretation of facts. True to its Greek spirit the modern West speaks of the victories of science over physical phenomena as a coveted prize that man wrenched from the hands of a mysterious Higher Power subjecting thereby nature to him gradually. It may also be perceived in the attitude of the modern West towards God. The only thing that makes man prostrate himself before God, it says, is his own sense of weakness. But each big stride that man takes forward in the various fields of science raises him to a higher plane of being — brings him nearer to godhood — till in the end he should be able to unravel all the mysteries of life , create life itself — an obsession of the modern scientist — and thus come on a par with that Being called God ! Then he will no longer feel compelled to prostrate himself before an unseen God, for he shall then himself be erected to the position of one.

This is the most dangerous malady that the modern West suffers from at present. It has poisoned all life. Humanity is torn and divided, one part set against the others. Peace, harmony and tranquility have become rare phenomena. But still there is one last hope: that is Islam. Let humanity turn towards this word of God, as this alone can save it from the doom brought on it by the Godless west. Islam equips man with a sound outlook upon life telling him that whatever knowledge he acquires or the material or spiritual benefits he enjoys, are in fact so many gifts of a Beneficent God to him. And that He is pleased with man so long as he employs the knowledge thus acquired in the service of mankind ; and that God of Islam does never get angry with His creatures for their aspiring after knowledge, nor does He have any fear whatsoever of them that they would challenge His authority or vie with Him; and that He is provoked to anger only when man abuses his knowledge of science and makes it a means to torment others or commits aggression against his fellowmen.

Thus Islam establishes not only peace and harmony but also rids mankind of tyranny and oppression. The contemporary world presents in this respect no better view than it did thirteen hundred years ago, when Islam freed it from all false gods. Tyranny still struts abroad in the guise of haughty kings, insolent demagogues and heartless capitalists who are busy as ever in sucking up the blood of the working millions, subjugating them and making capital out of their helplessness and miserable plight. There is still another class of dictators who rule with fire and sword, usurp peoples' liberties and go about chanting that they are merely instruments in enforcing the people's or the proletariat's will.

The assertion that Islam helps humanity shake off all of these shackles may occasion some readers to ask : why does not Islam then liberate its own followers from the oppressive tyranny of some of their rulers who have usurped all their liberties and exposed them to the most revolting forms of disgrace and dishonour in the very name of Islam ? To such readers we would like to point out that though these dictators exploit the name of Islam yet Islam is far from being in power in their domains or exercising any control or check over them. They belong to the class about which God Himself has declared that :

" And those who do not rule in accordance with what is revealed by God, are disbelievers." (5:44). Holy Quran

And that :

" But no ! By your Lord ! they do not believe (in reality) until they make you a judge of that which has become a matter of disagreement among them, and then do not find any straitness in their hearts as to what you have decided and submit with entire sub-mission." (4 : 65). Holy Quran.

The Islam that we call upon our fellowmen to adopt as their guide in life is not one and the same thing as that passed off under this name by some Muslim rulers of today's East. They have no respect or regard for the Divine Law as they seldom hesitate in breaking it at will. Thus when deciding their affairs they feel no need to be faithful to it following sometimes a man-made law borrowed from some European country and sometimes the Divine Law as may suit their needs or whims at the time. They are thus guilty of injustice towards both , towards men as well as God, for they choose from either side not what is right according to them but only that which might serve their personal ambitions, greed or lust.

The Islam that we know of is rather that which jolts down the haughty kings and insolent tyrants from above their proud seats of power. It makes them subject to the Divine Law along with other men and women or does away with them once for all, for " ....*As for the scum, it passes away as a worthless thing, and as for that which profits the people it tarries in the earth.*" (13 : 17). *The Holy Quran*

In the domain of this Islam and as a consequence thereof, there shall be no tyrants as it countenances no tyranny, nor does it allow any man to subjugate others or impose upon them his will, save that of God and His Apostle who command but that which is good and just. The ruler in such a community shall, as a part of his obligations to-wards men and God, be required to enforce Divine Law failing which he may no longer have any lawful claim to his subjects' obedience. They may in such a situation quite lawfully disregard his orders. This was explicitly stated by the first Caliph, Abu Bakr (may God be pleased with him) when he said that " Obey me only so long as I obey God with respect to you ; and if I should happen to deviate from

God's obedience, then in that case my obedience shall no longer be incumbent upon you." As such the ruler in Islam has no more right to tamper with the Public Exchequer or state legislation than the lowliest of his subjects. Moreover none would in such a domain of Islam have any right to rule others except after his election to a post of authority that the other members might have willingly devolved upon him in a free, just and impartial election with no checks on voters save those of justice, virtue and decency.

Such an Islamic State will not only liberate its citizens from all tyrants at home but shall safeguard their freedom against any outside aggression as well, whether it be in the form of imperialistic exploitation or a threat of it. This is so because Islam itself is a religion of glory and power and as such it cannot tolerate that men should degrade themselves by prostrating at the feet of the false God of imperialism. Islam prescribes a very simple code of life for man. It exhorts him to strive hard to gain the pleasure of his Creator, surrender his will to that of His, follow His commandments and come forward with all the sources at his disposal to fight against the damned spectre of imperialism and tyranny.

Let men therefore turn towards Islam for right

now is the time that all should flock together under its standard so as to sweep off from the face of the earth all the vestiges of imperialism. Therein lies the solitary hope of humanity of freeing itself from the clutches of this spectre that still clouds the world scene. Here is the way to real freedom such as allows of no serfdom, promises all men freedom in thought, action, property and religion jealously safeguarding their integrity as well as honour. For only thus can we become Muslims worthy of our God, the object of our adoration — in Whose path we tread, the path He chose for us : *"This day have I perfected for you religion and completed my favour on you and chosen for you Islam as religion."* (5:3). *The Holy Quran.*

Such a radical reformation effected by Islam is by no means a parochial one confined to the Muslim community alone, but is on the other hand by its very nature universal in character. It is nothing less than a blessing for the world of today afflicted as it is with internecine wars, with a still another and far more terrible third world war looming large on the horizon.

Today's world is divided into two big power blocs — the capitalist and the communist bloc, each set against the other in a deadly struggle for the capture of world-markets and important strategical points on the globe. They however, despite all their differences still remain one and the same thing as both are imperialistic in outlook and are out to enslave other peoples of the world. With this end in view they are both anxious to capture the maximum possible resources, human as well as material. Other human-beings are in their eyes no better than as so many chattels (Man-power they call it) or mere tools with which to realize their nefarious designs.

If the world of Islam should as a whole rise against the barbarous tyranny of the modern imperialist Powers — as it is in fact on the way to it — it can effectively end all international rivalries and bickerings that constitute so dangerous a threat for world security as well as peace. The Muslim countries can by closing their ranks very easily form a power block of their own. Thanks to its excellent geographical position such a power bloc of Muslim nations would hold the key to a balance of power in the comity of world nations, situated as it would be midways between the old and the new world. They will then be free to choose sides with this or that party in keeping with their own collective interests rather than serve those of the Eastern or the Western imperialism.

Islam is the only future hope of humanity ; and its victorious emergence out of the present ideological warfare is the only guarantee of man's salvation. But important as the triumph of Islam is for the future of mankind, its realization is also not a mere illusion. For, it can be effected if the people who are already in its folds and profess loyalty to it should right now pledge themselves for its glory and triumph. For this purpose they may not stand in need of any help whatever from outside. Such a triumph of Islam would, for the modern man, mean the abolition of the ever menacing shadows of an approaching world-wide conflagration ; it would mean no nervous break-downs, no physical or psychological tensions, in fact a happy home and a happy, peaceful world.

There is however yet another aspect of the matter too. The Modern West has achieved tre-mendous successes in the field of science, yet in the field of humanity it remains as savage and backward as ever. Under its dominance science advanced but man lagged far behind gradually losing all respect for the higher values in human life. Modern civiliza-tion stressed matter more than spirit, attached more importance to sensuality rather than spirituality with the result that the individuals have come to attach far more importance to their personal pleasures and selfish interests than strive or suffer for the common weal. That is why we find the modern man so engrossed in his sensual pleasures. Such a state of affairs can hardly be termed as man's progress or humanity's advancement, for it means not only material progress and scientific advancement but man's freedom from the dominance of his oppressive animal appetites as well. It is here that Islam steps in ; it alone can make man progress and be really advanced.

Progress is not synonymous to having fast moving planes, atom bombs, radios or dazzling electric lamps as some misguided people seem to think. These things offer no criterion to judge progress in human terms. The criterion of it would rather be : whether man is dominated over by his animal appetites or he controls and keeps them in check ? Has he the capacity to rise above these blind passions or is he a mere plaything in the hands of his unruly passions ? If he is still no better than a mere slave to them then he is far from having achieved any real progress or advancement. He may in such a case be rightly called a miserable failure as a man, notwithstanding his astounding conquests in the field of science and knowledge.

This criterion however is not an authoritative one arbitrarily fabricated by religion or morality. It is not a vision but a fact, to the veracity of which history bears ample witness as it is well grounded in the human nature and ultimate reality, for no people have ever been able to retain their strength, glory and power and contribute towards the welfare and advancement of human race once they fell a prey to the extravagances and luxuries of this life. What it was that brought the proud Greece of ancient times low ? and the Great Roman Empire ? How was it that the glory of ancient Persia and that of the Islamic world towards the end of the Abasside period faded out ? And lastly don't we still remember how the corrupt French Republic, with its people wholly engrossed in bodily pleasures fared in the last world war ? They surrendered to their enemies almost immediately. They could not withstand even a single blow of their enemy as they cared more for their personal pleasures than they were interested in the defence of their homeland. They were more concerned with the safeguard of their overpopulated Paris with its elegant dancing halls from the enemy shells than have any thought of redeeming the good name and honour of their once proud and brave nation.

At times America is also referred to by some misinformed people in the East as an example of a nation steeped in worldly pleasures, yet powerful and great with the highest material output in the world. But these people forget that America is yet a young nation in the spiritual as well as material sense of the word. And as all know youth is the period when the effects of an insidious disease are hardly detected, for the body-politic is still vigorous enough and fully capable of checking the outward manifestations of the disease. But a penetrating eye may not be deceived by the apparent health and youthful vigour of such a people, as it observes all the symptoms of the fatal malady distinctly and unmistakably behind the thin veil of its resplendent exterior. That America is no exception to the rule may be illustrated by the following two news items appearing in the papers sometime back. They also show that science despite all its progress is still as ineffectual as ever so far as effecting any basic change in human nature is concerned, for science is itself a part of God's Law — " the law wherein ye shall never witness a change."

The first news item describes that the State Department of America gave sack to thirty-three of its employees as they were found of a loose moral character and guilty of betraying state secrets to their enemies.

The second news-item purports to the effect that one hundred and twenty thousand American military men deserted the armed forces. This number is a fairly large one considering the total strength of the American armed forces and the fact that they belong to a nation still in its youth that also aspires for world leadership and domination.

This is just the beginning. The rest and the inevitable needs must follow if the American nation persists in its present materialistic attitude towards life.

However this is just one aspect of the picture. The other side shows that notwithstanding its highest material output, its relative youth and vast resources in men and land, the American nation has proved singularly barren in the world of principles and higher moral values due to the fact that, it is as a nation wholly engrossed in physical pleasures and in this respect has seldom been seen rising higher than the purely animal level. The savage treatment meted out to the negroes in the United States represents a nation spiritually unsound with a plane of humanity miserably low. Surely the world can never progress by stopping low for the gratification of animal appetites — by worshipping them.

This is indeed a very distressing picture of to-day's world but still there is one redeeming factor that is Islam. It freed mankind from the tyranny of animal appetites thirteen hundred years ago ; now again it is the only hope for mankind to shake off the shackles of lust and be free to direct all its faculties to reach a higher spiritual plane and propagate virtue and goodness in life.

Let none dare say that the revival of Islam is an impossible and hopeless undertaking, as the human race has in the past proved beyond any doubt that it is quite capable of rising above a purely animal level. And surely what once was possible in the past needs must still be possible in the present, for mankind has temperamentally not undergone any change ever since. The world of humanity sunk then as now, to quite as low level and was as much taken up with sensual pleasures as it at present seems to be. There is no difference between its present and past save the outwardly visible forms of voluptuousness or the names of the luxuries indulged in. Ancient Rome was no less rotten morally than its modern counterparts — Paris, London and the cities of America. Similarly in ancient Persia sexual anarchy was as rank as is at present associated with the communist countries. It was in this historical perspective that Islam was revealed to the world. It brought about a complete change, lifted mankind from the abyss of moral degradation, gave human life a lofty purpose, dynamism, movement and infused into it a spirit to strive hard in the way of truth and goodness. Humanity under Islam flourished, prospered and there was set afoot a dynamic intellectual and spiritual movement that encompassed the East as well as the West. No forces of evil and mischief dared check the onward march of Islam with the result that the whole outlook of human life was radically transformed. Thus the world of Islam became the headspring of light, excellence and progress in the world for a long time to come. During this long period of its dominance never did the Islamic world find itself lagging behind materially, intellectually or spiritually for the simple reason that it did not encourage moral corruption, sexual anarchy or Godlessness. Its followers were looked upon as symbols of goodness and excellence in all spheres of human activity till they ceased to reflect in their lives the noble and exalted ideals of Islam and became mere slaves to their whims and animal desires. It was then that all their glory and power came to an end in accordance with the immutable law of God.

The modern Islamic movement that is still gathering force derives its strength from the past and makes use of all the modern available resources with its gaze fixed on the future. It has great potentialities and as such has a bright future ahead, for it is fully capable of performing that great miracle which has once been already effected by Islam making man look higher and beyond animal pleasures —

with his feet planted firmly on earth and with his gaze fixed beyond the heavens.

This does not, however, mean that Islam is a mere spiritual creed, or a plea for morality, or just an intellectual research in the kingdom of heavens and earth. It is a practical code of life that fully embraces worldly affairs. Nothing escapes its penetrating eye. It takes notice of all the divers patterns of relationships binding men together irrespective of the fact that such relationships fall under the political, economical, or social heads ; regulates them by prescribing suitable laws and then enforces them in human life, the most outstanding characteristic of the performance being the achievement of a unique harmony between the individual and society, between reason and intuition, between practice and worship, between earth and Heavens, between this world and the Hereafter, all beautifully couched together in a single harmonious whole.

The space at our disposal in the present chapter is too limited to admit of any detailed discussion of the political, economical and social system of Islam. The following chapters will however throw some light on some of the salient features of this all comprehensive system of Islam in the course of dealing with the misunderstandings spread against it by the western scholars. The following facts we would however like to lay down here before our readers :

Firstly, it must be well understood that Islam is not a mere ideological vision. It is on the other hand a practical system of life that fully appreciates all the genuine needs of mankind and tries to realize them.

Secondly, in trying to meet the genuine requirements of man Islam effects a perfect balance so far as the limitations of human nature would allow. It starts with the individual maintaining a balance between his requirements of body and soul, reason and spirit and in no case allows one side to predominate the other. It does not suppress the animal instincts in order to make the soul ascend the higher planes, nor does it in hankering after the bodily desires, make man stoop down to the low level of mere animalism. On the other hand, it makes them both meet on a single higher plane doing away with all the internal psychological conflicts that threaten the entity of human soul or set a part of it against the other parts. Thence it proceeds to achieve an equilibrium between the needs of the individual and those of the community. It allows not an individual to transgress against other individuals, or the community.

Nor does it allow the community to commit transgression against the individual. It also does not approve of one class or people to enslave another class or people. Islam exercises a beneficent constraint on all these mutually opposed forces, prevents them from coming into collision with one another, calling upon them all to join hands, and co-operate for the general good of mankind as a whole.

Thus Islam strikes a balance between different factors of society, between spritual and temporal, economic and human factors. Unlike communism it does not believe that economic factors, *i.e.* the material aspect alone, dominate the human existence. Nor does it contribute to what the pure spiritualists or idealists say claiming that spiritual factors or high ideals alone are sufficient to organize human life. Islam rather holds that not one or two but all these divers elements put together form what is called human society ; and that the best code of life is that which takes note of all these, making full allowance for body as well as reason and spirit and arranging them all in the frame-work of a harmonious whole.

Thirdly, it must always be kept in mind that Islam has an altogether independent existence of its own as a social philosophy as well as an economic system. Some of its outward manifestations may on the surface appear to resemble those of capitalism or communism, but in fact it is far from being the one or the other. It retains all the good characteristics of these systems yet is free from their shortcomings and perversions. It extols not individualism to that loathful extent which is characteristic of the modern West that holds the individual as the basis of social order and says that freedom of the individual must in all circumstances be preserved and in no case interfered with by the community. From this germ sprang up in the West the modern capitalism that is based on the concept of the individual's freedom to exploit others including the community that upbrings and preserves him. Islam, while emphasising the importance of society, does not go to the extreme such as is witnessed in the countries of Eastern Europe. They hold society the basis of human life wherein the individual is no more than an insignificant midget with no existence whatever of its own outside and independent of the herd. Therefore, the community alone enjoys freedom as well as power ; the individual has no right to question its authority or demand of it his rights. Thus did there originate communism claiming that the state holds the absolute powers to shape, howsoever it should desire, the lives of the individuals.

Islam strikes a balance between these two extremes — communism and capitalism. Recognizing the importance of both it so harmonises the individual and the state that individuals have the freedom necessary to develop their potentialities but not to transgress against others of their fellowmen, as also it gives to the community or the state that represents the organized community — vast powers to regulate and control the socio-economic relationships — so as ever to guard and maintain this harmony in human life. The basis of this whole structure as envisaged by Islam is the reciprocity of love between individuals and groups ; it is not erected on the basis of malevolence and class conflict as the communist societies.

It may also be pointed out here that this unique system of life as envisaged by Islam, did not originate as a result of any economic pressure, nor was it an outcome of some mutually conflicting interests of antagonistic groups of people. No, not only this but it was revealed to the world as the ordained system of life at a time when men attached no particular importance to the economic factors, nor did they know anything about social justice in the sense we know it in modern times. Both communism and capitalism are much latter growths. As far as a reformation in the social and economic spheres of the human life is concerned, the basic needs of man — food, housing, and sexual satisfaction — with which the name of Karl Marx is generally associated as being the first to hold that it was the duty of the government to make provision for these basic needs of man. This is claimed as a great revolution in the history of human thought. But long before Karl Marx — thirteen hundred years ago — Islam had already proclaimed these very rights of the individual before the world. Thus the Holy Prophet (peace be upon him) said that : " *Whosoever acts as a public officer for us (i.e. the Islamic State) and has no wife, he shall have a wife : if he has no house, he shall be given a house to live in ; if he has no servant, he shall have one ; and if he has no animal (a conveyance), he shall be provided with one.*" This historical announcement of the fundamental human rights not only includes those voiced by Karl Marx, but it adds to them some more as well, without however necessitating any inter-class hatred, bloody revolutions, and without of course, rejecting all those human elements in life that do not fall under the above three heads : food, housing and sexual surfeit.

These are some of the salient features of the Islamic code of life. They are sufficient to prove that a religion with such laws and principles, and so comprehensive as to include the whole of the human existence, emotions, thoughts, actions, worship, economic dealings, social relationships, instinctive urges and spiritual aspirations — all arranged in the framework of a single harmonious but unique system of life, can never lose its usefulness for mankind. Nor can such a religion ever become obsolete as its objectives are the same as those of life itself and therefore destined to live on so long as there is life on this planet.

Considerig the existing state of affairs in the contemporary world, mankind cannot reasonably afford to turn its back upon Islam or reject its system of life. Mankind is still afflicted with the most savage and odious forms of racial prejudices in even this so-called enlightened twentieth century. America and South Africa may offer a case in point in this respect. Surely the twentieth century world has yet a great deal to learn from Islam. Long ago Islam freed humanity from all racial prejudices. It did not content itself with the presentation of a beautiful vision of equality alone but in practice did also achieve an unprecedented state of equality between all people, black, white or red declaring that none enjoyed any priority over the others except in virtue of piety. It not only freed the black from slavery but also fully recognized their rights to aspire even to the highest seat of authority in the Islamic State. They could like freemen become the heads of the Islamic State. The Holy Prophet (peace be upon him) said: " *Listen and obey even if a negro slave be appointed as your superior so long as he should enforce amongst you the Law of God.*"

How can also the world of today ignore the message of Islam stricken as it is with the evils of imperialism and tyranny with all their barbarous attributes, for Islam alone can help mankind shake off their chains. It is opposed to imperialism and all forms of exploitation. The treatment of Islam with the peoples of the countries it conquered with a view to spread the word of God, was so generous, lofty and sublime that the eyes of the pygmies of the " Civilized " Europe can hardly penetrate those heights. We may in this regard cite the famous decision of the Caliph, Omar bin Al Khattab to whip the son of Amr ibnil-Aas, the victorious general and honoured governor of Egypt as he had beaten an Egyptian Copt without any legal justification with the renowned father himself having a very narrow escape from the whip of the Caliph. This shows how great civil liberty was enjoyed by the subjects of the Islamic State.

Then there is the evil of capitalism that has poisoned all life. Its abolition and the need to rid human race of its evil consequences again calls for Islam. For, Islam prohibits usury and hoarding which taken together form the mainstay of the capitalist economy. This in other words means that Islam alone can effectively check the evils of capitalism as it did check them thirteen hundred years ago.

Similarly the world dominated over by the materialistic, godless communism cannot help standing in need of Islam as it achieves and maintains social justice of the highest order without recourse to drying up the spiritual head-springs in human heart. Nor does it confine man's world to the narrow world of the senses. Above all it neither endeavours nor aims at the imposition of its own creed on mankind forcibly with the iron rod of a proletarian dictatorship, for, *"There is no compulsion in religion; indeed the righteousness has been differentiated from wickedness."* (*Holy Quran* 2:256)

Finally, the world with the shadows of war still hanging over it cannot but turn towards Islam — the only way to establish and maintain real peace on this earth.

The era of Islam has in a way just started, not ended ; it is not a spent force, but a living dynamic force. Its future is as bright as its great historical past is glorious when it illumined the face of earth at the time when Europe was still groping its way in the dark recesses of medievalism.

The Holy Quran states : " *And such of your slaves as seek a writing (of emancipation), write it for them if ye are aware of aught of good in them, and bestow upon them of the wealth of Allah which He hath bestowed upon you.*" (*24 : 33*)

ISLAM AND SLAVERY

Perhaps this is the most odious form of doubt exploited by the Communists in order to shake the faith of the Muslim youth in his religion, Islam. If Islam were suited to every period of human history, it would not, as it did, approve of slavery, which proves conclusively that Islam was but meant for a limited period of history only. It has fulfilled its mission and now stands outmoded and obsolete, for it was not designed to be a religion for all times and climes.

The sincere Muslim youth is also haunted by similar doubts. Why did Islam permit slavery ? This religion is no doubt revealed by God ; there can be no doubt about that, and that it was revealed for the good of the whole of mankind for all times to come, but how is it that it allowed slavery ? How did the religion based on the notion of perfect equality among men, stressing the common origin of them all and then successfully translating its concept of equality in its social life recognize slavery as a part of its social system and as such made laws for it ? Does God intend that human beings for ever should remain divided as masters and slaves ? Does He want that the human race should continue to have a group of people among them that is sold and bought as chattel as was the case with the slaves, when He Himself said of human beings : " *And surely we have dignified the children of Adam,*" and if God did not intend or like that, why did He not then explicitly forbid it in His Book and abolish it outright as He did for instance, abolish drinking, gambling, and usury etc., the practices which He abhorred ? In short the Muslim youth knows that Islam is a true religion but like Abraham he is perplexed and seems to be in a state of mind described in the Quranic verse :

> " *And when Abraham said, My Lord, show me how You give life to the dead, He said : What ! and do you not believe ? He said : Yes, but that my heart may be at ease.*" *The Holy Quran* (2 :260)

As against this the youth, whose reason is impaired and beliefs confused by the imperialistic machinations does not wait for the truth to be made clear before him but is swept away by his passions and without any inclination to inquire into the reality jumps to the conclusion that Islam is antiquated and hence, is no longer needed by man.

The Communists, who hoodwink people by claiming to be scientific, trade in ideas borrowed from their masters abroad which they arrogantly parade giving a false impression of having discovered an unalterable and eternal truth, the genuineness of which cannot be challenged, nor contradicted. The truth they claim to have discovered is the dialectical materialism — the theory which states that human life is divided into certain definite economic phases such as can neither be avoided, nor passed by mankind viz. first communism, slavery, feudalism, capitalism and the second communism (deemed to be the last page in the book of history) and that all creeds, disciplines, and thoughts that human history knows of were in fact mere reflection of the various economic conditions or economic systems that prevailed at different periods of human history. These past creeds and beliefs were all right for those bygone ages, for they fully co-ordinated with the economic structure and circumstances of those times but they can never be suitable for the next higher stages of human development as these are always based on a quite new and a different pattern of economy. Hence, they conclude, that there can be no single system of life such as could be suitable for all times to come. Now as Islam came to the world at a time when the stage of slavery was coming to an end and that of feudalism just beginning, it brought with itself laws, creeds and a discipline of life all of which were in concord with the prevalent circumstances of economic existence. That is why it approved of slavery as well as permitted feudalism, for Islam could not anticipate the next stage of economic development nor give any system to the world for which the economic conditions were not yet ripe, for, as the Blessed Lord Karl Marx said, it was absolutely impossible.

We intend to discuss this problem of slavery in its historical, social as well as psychological context with an open mind and without allowing ourselves to be hoodwinked by the clamours of these tricksters and so-called scientific scholars.

———————

When a modern man looks at the problem of slavery with his twentieth century background and in the light of the hideous crimes perpetrated during the slave trade and the abominably barbarous treatment that was meted out to slaves (especially in the Roman Empire) he discovers it as a most shocking and horrid crime. He is at a loss and finds it extremely difficult to understand as to how such a thing could be approved of by a religion or a system of life. He wonders: how could Islam allow slavery when all its other laws and principles point out towards the freedom of man from all types and forms of slavery ! and then overwhelmed by a sense of shame he desires :

would that Islam had set our hearts and minds at ease by banning slavery in clear, explicit terms ! !

Let us pause here awhile and see as to what story the historical facts have got to tell us. The fact is that the hideous crimes committed against the slaves in the Roman Empire are quite foreign to the Islamic history. We have got ample evidence with regard to the life the slaves in the Roman world led which is quite sufficient to illustrate the great change brought about by Islam in their fate.

The slave in the Roman world was considered a mere " commodity " and not a human being. He had no rights whatsoever although he was en-cumbered with cumbrous duties and obligations. And whence did these slaves come? They were captured in wars, which were not initiated by any noble principe or lofty ideals but were solely directed by their wish to enslave other peoples and exploit them for their own self-aggrandizement. These wars were waged in order to enable the Roman people indulge in licentious luxuries and live in prosperity, enjoy cold and hot baths, costly costumes, delicious and tasty foods of every kind, and revel in sensual pleasures — drinking bouts, whoredom, dancing as well as public gatherings and festivals. In order to provide for these enjoyments they subjugated other nations and exploited them most mercilessly. Egypt that was freed from the Roman overlordship by Islam was treated no less cruelly. It constituted a granary of wheat for the Roman empire, besides furnishing various kinds of other material resources.

To satisfy this greedy lust of the Roman imperialists the slaves toiled for them in the fields. As mentioned above they enjoyed no rights. When working in the fields they were fettered in heavy manacles so as to prevent their running away. They were never fed properly but given just sufficient to keep them alive and fit to do their work, and this too not because they thought it was their right to be provided for with sustenance as even the beasts and trees are. During the work they were whipped just for the savage pleasure of it which was much relished by their sadist lord or his agent. At the end of the day large groups of them — from ten to fifty men a group and still fettered in their manacles — were herded together to sleep in dark foul smelling cells infested with mice and insects. They were denied even the comfort of wide and spacious folds such as are enjoyed by cattle in their enclosures.

But the worst and most revolting feature of the Roman attitude towards these slaves was represented by what formed their best loved diversion which by the way also brings into light the innate barbarous and inhuman character of the Roman civilization — the civilization which is in modern times represented by modern Europe and America with all the means of imperialistic exploitation at their disposal. The slaves carrying swords and lances were led out into the arenas with their masters and occasionally the emperor himself seated around exalted seats in order to watch them fight, in dead earnest, for their diversion. The slaves fell upon one another with their swords and spears, recklessly hacking themselves to pieces. The climax was reached when someone of the fighters killed a fellow slave and threw him cold and lifeless on the ground. At this he was lustily applauded with loud hurrahs, vigorous hand clappings and joyous, hearty laughter.

This was how the slaves fared in the Roman world. We need not dwell upon their legal position in this set-up : the absolute right of the master to kill, punish or exploit them mercilessly without any right on their part to complain even, and without expecting any moral support whatever from any quarter, as it would add little to our knowledge after going over all that we have in brief described above.

The slave was no better off than this in Persia, India and other countries. Despite all their minor differences the fate of the slave remained the same among all these nations : his life had no worth, his murder no retaliation; he was burdened with cumbersome obligations carrying with them little or no rights in return. The systems prevalent in these countries differed neither in intent, nor in content with regard to the slaves ; they differed merely in the degree or intensity of their cruelty and hideousness which they betrayed in their attitudes towards slaves.

Such were the conditions of life that obtained when Islam arrived at the scene. Its advent heralded the restoration of human dignity to these slaves. It told the masters as to their slaves : " *You are (sprung) the one from the other* "[1] It proclaimed that : *He who kills his slave, we shall kill him ; who mutilates his nose, we shall cut his nose ; and who gelds our slave, we shall get him gelded in return.* [2]" It recognized a common descent, abode as well as return for all men, master and slave alike saying : "*you are all sons of Adam and Adam was created from dust* [3]," and stressed that there was no superiority for a master over his slave merely because of his being a master : whatever superiority there was, it rested

---

1. The Holy Quran (4 : 25.)
2. Al-Hadith, narrated by both Bukhari & Muslim besides Abu Daud, Tirmidhi and Nisai.
3   Al Hadith. Muslim & Abu Daud.

on piety : " *There is no superiority for an Arab, nor for a black man over a red one, nor for a red over a blackman save due to piety.*[1]".

Islam came and told the masters that they should be fair and good in their dealings with the slaves : " *And be good to the parents and to the near of kin and the orphans and the needy and the neighbour of (your) kin and the alien neighbour and the companion in a journey and the wayfarer and those whom your right hand possesses ; surely Allah does not love him who is proud, boastful.*"[2] It stressed the fact that the true relationship between the master and his slave was not one of slavery and overlordship, nor of subjection or objection but that of kinship and brotherhood. Thus the masters were permitted to marry the slave-girls they had in their possession: " *... Let them marry from the believing maids whom your right hands possess. Allah knoweth best (concerning) your faith. Ye (proceed) one from another ; so wed them by premission of their folk, and give unto them their portions in kindness,*" The Holy Quran (4 : 25).

Thus the masters were described as brothers to their slaves : " *Your slaves are your brothers .... so he who has a brother under him should feed him and clothe him as he himself feeds and dresses ; do not ask them do things which are beyond their power and if you do ask them to do such things then help them* [3]."

---

1.   Bukhari.
2.   The Holy Quran   (4 : 36.
3.   Al Hadith.

With a mark of deference to the feelings of the slaves the Holy Prophet added : " *None of you should say : this is my slave and this is my slave-girl ; he should rather say : This is my man and this is my maiden* [1] " It was on this authority that Abu Huraira on seeing a man riding a horse and his slave trudging along after him, said to the man : " Get him seated on the horse behind you, for, surely he is your brother, and his soul is similar to yours."

This was, however, not all that Islam did for the slaves, but before proceeding with our inquiry, we would first like to sum up the great advance that thanks to Islam came about in the position of the slave at this preliminary stage.

The slave was now no longer regarded just a commodity — a merchandize — but was looked upon as a human being with a soul similar to that of his master, whereas in the past he was regarded as a being, quite different from his master and created to serve as a slave in every way fit to suffer humiliation. It was because of this notion that their consciences never twinged them when murdering, punishing, cauterizing or making their slaves perform loath-

---

I.   Hadith narrated by Abu Huraira.

some and burdensome jobs [1]. Islam raised them from this state of abject slavery to the exalted status of brotherhood with free men. These achievements of Islam were not mere professions but a fact to which history bears witness. Even the prejudiced writers of Europe too admit that in the early period of Islam the slave was exalted to such a noble state of humanity as never before was witnessed in any other part of the world. They won so dignified a status within the Muslim community as made the freed slaves abhor betraying their erstwhile masters although now they stood in no need or fear of them and were now as free as they. The reason for this lay in the fact that they considered themselves to be members of the family of their previous masters and linked to them with ties akin to those of blood.

Also the slave now came to be regarded as a human being whose personal safety was guaranteed by law not permitting the commission of any transgression against him through word or act. As to the word, the Prophet

---

1. The Hindus (India) believed that the slaves (the Sudras) had sprung from the feet of the God and hence they assumed that they were innately mean and low, a fate they could never contend or change. Therefore the only way open before them was that they should suffer this humiliation and chastisement patiently in the hope that their souls may after their death transmigrate into a better creation. Thus their oppressors not content with reducing them to the wretched state of physical slavery proceeded further to deprive them even of the will to rise in revolt against the unjust social order that subjected them to humiliation and misery.

forbade the Muslims to talk of their slaves as such and instead commanded them to address them in a manner that should make them think of themsleves as members of their family, and blot out from their persons the stigma of slavery. With this in view he said : *" Surely God has made you their masters ; and if He had willed He could have likewise given you in their possession as slaves* [1] " This means that it was the particular conditions and circumstances that had made them slaves, otherwise they were as good as their masters. In this way Islam deflated a little the swollen pride of the masters along with raising the status of slaves so as to connect them all in a purely human relationship. It brought them closer and fostered love among them telling them that love and nothing else should form the basis of all their mutual relationships. In the case of physical harm or injury for both of them a kindred punishment was explicitly laid down. *" He who slays his slave we shall put him to death,"* is a principle very clear in its vast implications, all of which go to show that a state of perfect equality prevailed between the slave and his master as between one man and another, besides guaranteeing to both of them the right to live as human beings. Thus Islam made it clear that the present situation — slavery — did not preclude them from their rights

---

I.   For reference please see Ghazali's Ihya-Uloom-i-Din' chapter on Rights of Slaves.

as human beings. These guarantees not only were quite sufficient to grant a slave his safety and security of life but they were so generous and noble that no other parallel in the whole history of slave laws exists at all either before or after the advent of Islam. In this respect Islam went to such an extent that it forbade the master to even slap his slave, except for the purposes of correction (which has its own prescribed limits that may neither be passed by nor overlooked under any circumstances, the punishment given being however, similar to the punishment the master may award his own children on their mischiefs). This also provided a legal justification for setting the slaves at liberty. And with this we pass on to the next stage — the stage of actual enfranchisement.

In the first stage Islam gave spiritual enfranchisement to slaves. It gave them back their humanity and taught that from the standpoint of a common origin they enjoyed a status similar to that of their masters and that it was the external circumstances alone that had deprived them of their freedom, preventing them thereby to participate directly in the social life of the community. But for this only point of difference, there was no other difference between slaves and masters as far as their rights as human. beings were concerned.

But Islam did not stop short there as the great fundamental principle of it is the achievement of a perfect equality among all men making everyone of them equally free. Therefore it proceeded to bring about the actual freedom of the slaves by two important means : (1) voluntary emancipation by the masters (Al Itq) and (2) writing of their freedom (Mukatabah)

(I) : As to the first of these (i.e. Al Itq.) it was a voluntary act on the part of the master to set a slave at liberty. The practice was greatly encouraged by Islam and the Holy Prophet himself in this regard too provided the best example for his followers. He freed all the slaves he had. His companions followed his example, Abu Bakr in particular, spending large sums of money on buying off slaves from the idolatrous chiefs of Quraish to set them free later on. Besides this the slaves were also bought out of the Public Exchequer whenever there was some money to spare for this purpose so as to set them free. Yahya bin Saeed says : ' Umar bin Abdul Aziz sent me to collect alms from Africa. I collected the alms and then looked for the poor to distribute the alms among them but I found none, nor I found anyone who might have accepted them from me, for, Umar bin Abdul Aziz had enriched the people. So I bought a slave with the money and then set him free.''

The Holy Prophet used to free a slave who would teach reading and writing to ten Muslims or render

any other kindred service to the Muslim community.
The Quran enjoined that atonement for some of the
sins consisted in freeing of slaves as also the holy
Prophet encouraged it for the reparation of any other
sin one might commit. This contributed more than
anything to bring liberty to the greatest number of
slaves, for, no man could hope to be wholly free from
sin as the Holy Prophet said : *" All sons of Adam
are sinners."* It may be well to point out here one of
the atonements prescribed by Islam for sins, as it in
particular illustrates the standpoint of Islam with
regard to slavery. Islam prescribed that redemption
for the killing of a believer by mistake was the freeing
of a believing slave and paying blood money to his
people : *" And whoever kills a believer by mistake, he
should free a believing slave, and blood-money should be
paid to his people* [1] *".* The murdered man killed
by mistake, was a human being of whose services
his people as well as the community was deprived without any legal justification, for which
reason Islam prescribed that a compensation should
be made to both parties, his people and the society :
his people getting a just blood-money and the society
another man to serve it in his place, the newly
freed believing slave. Thus the freeing of a slave meant
bringing back to life a human being as a compensa-

I.   The Holy Quran (4 : 92.)

tion for the one who was lost due to his being killed by mistake. As is clear from this, Islam views slavery as death or a state very much similar to it notwithstanding all those securities that it did provide for a slave. That is why it eagerly snatched at every opportunity to resuscitate this wretched class of human beings by restoring to them their liberty.

History tells us that such large numbers of slaves achieved their freedom through this voluntary emancipation (Al Itq) in Islam as have no other parallel in the history of any other nation, before or after Islam till modern times, besides the fact that the factors that contributed towards this emancipation were purely humane springing up from Muslims' sincerest wish to win their God's pleasure by freeing the slaves they possessed.

(2) The second means whereby Islam brought freedom to slaves was that of Mukataba *i.e.* the writing of freedom to a slave on his asking for it by the master in return for a certain amount of money agreed upon by both of them. The master could in such a case neither refuse, nor delay the freeing of a slave ready to ransom his freedom ; he needs must set him at liberty on the reception of the ransom. Otherwise the slave could move the court to decree his enfranchisement.

By this institution of Mukatabah, Islam paved the way for the freedom of all those slaves, who happened to desire their freedom and not passively wait for their masters' good will or piety to set them at liberty at their own convenience.

From the moment a slave offered to ransom his freedom, not only his master could not turn down the offer, but there was also no need for him to fear any repercussions, for the Islamic Government guaranteed that he would henceforth work for his master in return for a fixed payment, or would make arrangements for him to work outside for anyone else on hire till the time he is able to collect the money needed for the winning back of his freedom.

This was what happened in Europe afterwards in the fourteenth century that is, some seven centuries after Islam had already enforced it in its domain. The great distinguishing feature of Islam that is hardly to be looked for anywhere else, was the financial aid the Islamic Government advanced to slaves such as would demand the writing of their freedom out of the Public Exchequer. This was a clear manifestation of the great interest Islam had in the voluntary emancipation of slaves without expecting any material gains in return, merely with a view to secure God's pleasure and fulfil one's obligations as a slave towards Him. The Quranic verse describing the uses of poor-rate (Az-Zakat) says : " *Alms are only for the poor and the needy, and the officials (appointed) over them .... and the (ransoming of) captives.*" (9 : 60). Thus the Quran laid it down that the poor-rate (Az-Zakat) should be spent for purchasing the freedom of such slaves as were unable to work out their own liberty with the help of their personal earnings.

These two institutions in Islam signified a great practical advancement achieved by Islam in the history of slavery. It forestalled the normal historical advancement of mankind by at least seven centuries, besides featuring some quite new ingredients of advancement such as the security afforded by the state to the slave — something rare in the history of mankind till modern times — and others which mankind is far from having yet realized *e.g.* the noble and generous treatment of slaves, or freeing them of one's own free will without any external pressure of economic or political developments such as at last forced the peoples of Europe to grant freedom to slaves.

These two things are sufficient to confute the false assertions of the Communists, who claim that all systems including Islam represent but a particular stage in the economic development of mankind. Faithful to the law of dialectical materialism thus

Islam too with all its beliefs, and views came at a time best suited for it, reflecting the economic and material conditions of the period, for a system may according to them, only reflect the economic life but can by no means anticipate a future economic stage. They insist that this theory cannot be false as it has been testified by the Reason of the One who " *can neither be influenced with falsehood from above nor from below* " — the Reason of Karl Marx, the most Exalted and Blessed one ! But the bottom is knocked out of this falsehood by Islam — a standing refutation of all this Marxist humbug, for it did not work up its way in the manner Marx prescribed, inside the Arabian peninsula, nor outside it all the world over. And this is true not only with regard to the life of slaves under Islam but is equally tenable in its manner of distributing wealth, in determining the mutual relationship of the ruler and the ruled, and of a master's to his hireling. [1] On the other hand Islam raised its whole social and economic superstructure on voluntary obedience of such a style as in many ways still remains unsurpassed and unmatched in the history of social systems.

Here a very perplexing question may haunt some persons: Why is it that Islam — so great a champion of slave emancipation and taking such radical steps towards that end voluntarily and without any outside

---

[1]. Please also see the next chapter.

pressure or coercion before all the world, did not also take the final and decisive step, and abolish it once for all, as it might have in that way immensely benefited mankind besides proving thereby that it was really a system most perfect and in effect revealed by God, who dignified the sons of Adam over many of his creations ?

For an answer to this question we need must inquire into the allied social, psychological and political problems of slavery — the reasons due to which Islam delayed its much expected and outright abolition. We must also during this inquiry bear in mind that actually the abolition of slavery was rather delayed more than Islam would have desired or allowed it if it had continued functioning properly in its pristine purity, unadulterated by extraneous ingredients of deviation.

In the first place then it must be recorded that when Islam came, slavery was prevalent throughout the world as an acknowledged fact of socio-economic existence. There was hardly a man to be met with who was repelled by it, or who felt any need for a change. As such the changing or the total discarding of it required a gradual process stretched over a long period of time. Thus we see that prohibition of liquor was effected not immediately but after years of preliminary preparation although it before all other things constituted a mere individual habit, notwithstanding the fact that it carried so many social implications as well and that some of the Arabs practised abstinence even in the days of ignorance, believing it a vice degrading for a truly noble man. But slavery was looked upon by them as something quite different. It was deep-rooted in the social structure of the times as well as the psychology of the individuals, as it entailed individual as well as social and economical implication and as we observed above nobody regarded its existence as something undesirable. That is why its abolition required a period of time far longer than the life of the Holy Prophet, the period which coincided with the period of divine revelation through him. God, the Best Knower of all that He created, knew that the total prohibition of wine would be achieved after a few years by a mere commandment. So He did command its prohibition when such time came. Similarly if the conditions of life had been such as a mere direction were to suffice to suppress the evil of slavery, God Almighty would have expressly forbidden it once for all without any further delay.

When we say that Islam is a religion for all mankind and for all times, and that it embraces in itself all the healthy elements necessary for the existence and continuance of good life, we do not at all mean that it has once for all laid down all the detailed rules for all times and climes. No, that is not so, for it has given such detailed directions only with regard to those basic human problems only that remain unaltered through all the different vicissitudes of history, for the roots of these problems lie deep in the unchangeable instinctive headsprings of human nature. As to the ever changing conditions of life, Islam is content with laying down some general principles for them so as to outline their future course of development. This is precisely what it did with respect to the problem of slavery ; it laid down a sound basis for the freeing of slaves, through voluntary enfranchisement or by the ransoming of their freedom, besides pointing out the course to a permanent resolution of this old and complicated problem in future.

Islam did not mean to change human nature. It rather sought to civilize it making due allowance for its inevitable limitations so as to help it ascend the highest possible planes of perfection without any recourse to suppression or repression. It recorded a miraculous success in transforming some individuals. As regards human society as a whole its success was no less glorious ; it bears no analogy to anything else ever achieved in the domain of human history. But despite all this it did not aim at transmuting human beings to a degree of perfection both rare as well as impossible in practical life of human beings with all their present human limitations. For, if God had intended that, He would have from the very first created men like angels and as such ordered them to bear burdens that can be borne by angels only, of whom it is said that : *"They do not disobey God in all that He orders them ; and they do what they are commanded to."*[1] God did not intend to transmute men into angels such as these ; He rather made them men and as such He knows their potentialities and the time necessary for their flourishing so as to enable them to follow and successfully execute an order. However it is quite sufficient for Islam to be the first to initaite the emancipation movement which took the world some seven centuries to adopt and enforce. The fact nonetheless is that Islam had before long practically put an end to slavery in the Arabian peninsula and but for the presence of a new headspring of slavery due to which slavery lingered on every where in the world, it was quite capable of undertaking in earnest its similar effacement in the whole world of Islam. In the presence of this new cause of servitude it was not possible for Islam to abolish it outright, for it concerned not only the Muslims but their opponents as well on whom Islam exercised no control or power. The source that thus prevented the total effacement of slavery was war,

---

1. The Holy Quran (66 : 6)

the most fruitful source of slavery at the time. We would discuss it shortly in some detail.

In treating slaves well and restoring their human status Islam has left behind some most wonderful and admirable examples. Of these we have already referred to some of the Quranic verses and traditions of the Holy Prophet. Here we would in brief take some more examples from practical life in the early period. When in Madina, the Holy Prophet established brotherhood between some Arab chiefs and some freed slaves. Thus he joined as brothers Bilal son of Rabah and Khalid son of Ru-waihata Al Khas'ami, Zaid, the freed slave of the Prophet and Hamza, the uncle of the Prophet, and Kharijah son of Zaid and Abu Bakr. This relationship of brotherhood was a real bond akin to the blood-relationship, so much so that the two persons thus made brothers inherited from each other just as only the blood relations now do.

But Islam did not stop at that. It went a step further. Thus the Prophet married his cousin Zainab, daughter of Jahsh to his ex-slave Zaid. But marriage touches a very delicate aspect of a person's life especially in that of a woman. Therefore although Zainab accepted a man far below her in social status, she could not reconcile herself to be the wife of one who did not come of a noble family like her, nor possessed wealth. But the Holy Prophet did by this act set an example to show how a slave could attain to the highest level of a Qureishite chief from out of the abyss of ignominy into which he was hurled by his cruel fellow human beings. But still this did not satisfy Islam.

Slaves were exalted to the position of military commanders and leaders. Thus when the Holy Prophet sent out an army which consisted of the closest of the Companions—Emigrants and the Helpers, the acknow-edged leaders of the Arabs - he entrusted Zaid, the slave, with the generalship of the army. After the death of Zaid the Holy Prophet appointed his son, Osama as the commander of the army consisting of such illustri-ous men as Abu Bakr and Omar, his two principal ministers and afterwards successors. Thus slaves were given not only a status equal and similar to others but were at the same time raised to the exalted positions of heading the armies of free men. In this regard the Holy Prophet went to such a great length that he is reported to have commanded the believers : " *Hear and obey (the orders of Your leaders) although the man appointed above you as your leader be a negro slave with a raisin-like head so long as he continues to enforce among you God's law.*[1]" Thus even a slave could aspire to the highest office in the Islamic state. When faced with the problem of appointing his successor, Omar said : " Had Salim, the slave of Abi Huzaifa been alive, I would have appointed him caliph." This was just a continuation of the tradition founded by the Holy Prophet.

Omar's life affords a yet another admirable instance bearing upon the respect enjoyed by slaves in the Muslim society. When he was vehemently opposed by Bilal, son of Rabah, an ex-slave, concerning the problem of Fay (conquered lands) Omar despairing of all other means of silencing his opposition prayed to God : " My God ! Requite me with Bilal and his comrades ! " What a reaction for a caliph in the face of opposition by one of ex-slaves from among his subjects.

The great superiority of Islam with regard to slavery is manifest in various aspects. It aimed at freeing slaves externally as well as internally but to achieve that end did not merely rely upon the pious wishes as Abraham Lincoln had done by issuing an order without preparing slaves mentally. This demonstrates Islam's deep understanding of the human nature and how it employed all possible means to achieve its objective. It not only liberally restored

I. Bukhari.

these people's liberty but also trained them so as to safeguard it and bear responsibilities flowing from it. It infused a spirit of love and co-operation throughout the society. It did not wait till conflicts should break out within the society over these rights as had happened in Europe leaving behind them an odious legacy of bitter malice and hatred and sapping all the spiritual headsprings in human heart. In the end let us now take up the main basis on which Islam worked out the final emancipation after a due process of spiritual elevation of slaves.

We have already pointed out that Islam successfully put an end to all those old sources whence slavery sprang up save one, which it was virtually impossible for it to do away with, and that was war, the only effective source of this evil left behind after the crusade of Islam against it. We propose to deal with it at some length.

The principal practice that dated back to the remotest past and was prevalent at the time was that prisoners of war were either enslaved or put to death. [1]

I. On page 2273 of the Historical Encyclopaedia called ,' Universal History of the World'' we are told that in the year 599 A.D., the Roman emperor Marius motivated by his love for economy refused to ransom a few of the millions of those prisoners that had been captured by his forces in wars. He instead put them all without a single exception to sword.

It was a practice such as had with the passage of time come to stay as a necessary condition of human existence in those past ages.

It was against this social background that Islam was revealed to mankind. Many battles took place between the forces of Islam and its opponents. The Muslims taken prisoners in these wars were made slaves by their captors. Their liberties were forefeited, Men were exposed to oppression and all those miseries that were commonly the lot of a slave at the time. The honour of the woman was violated in a most flagrant manner ; several men, fathers, sons and friends all jointly shared a single captive woman with no regard whatever to any rule or law, or respect for her womanhood, or any consideration whatever about her being a virgin maid or a married woman. Besides this the children, if captured, were brought up in a most odious and abject servitude.

As the conditions stood it was not possible for Islam to forthwith set at liberty all the prisoners falling in its hands from the camp, for it would have not only been a piece of bad policy but would have also implied a virtual encouragement to its enemies especially as the Muslims as well as their dear and near ones captured in war were being made slaves by the enemies and exposed to all sorts of tortures, atrocities and humiliations. In such circumstances the best and the only course left open before Islam was to treat them as captives as they treated the Muslims. The enslaving of the prisoners of war could not be abolished unilaterally by Islam when the enemies insisted on its continuance. So the practice was tolerated just so long as there did exist no alternative to it and till the time that the peoples all the world over should agree among themselves upon a basis other than that of slavery in dealing with their prisoners of war. We must not also overlook the great difference between Islam and other religions in their wars or the treatment of the prisoners captured in these wars.

The wars have been and still are a melee of treachery, surprise, violence and the enslavement of one nation to another due to its expansionist designs and the lust for exploitation in order to advance its own selfish ends. Such wars are and have been the outcome of a personal ambition, pride, vanity or a wish for vengeance of a king or a military commander. Motivated as these wars were by low earthly designs, the people captured in them were made slaves not because of their creed or ideal, nor because they were inferior in their physical, psychological or intellectual equipment to that of their captors, but simply because they had lost the battle and belonged to the vanquished party. Moreover there was nothing that could in the event of war, prevent a victorious party to subject the conquered people to humiliation and disgrace, violate their honour, raise the peaceful cities to the ground and put the women, children as well as the old men to sword, — a logical sequence to lack of a lofty ideal, principle or creed to guide them.

With the advent of Islam all these practices were abolished. It prohibited all wars save the one fought in the way of God ; to avert cruelty and injustice to Muslims ; crush a tyrannous oppressor resorting to force and violence to prevent people from embracing true religion ; or to remove a powerful but iniquitous imposter interposing between men and their God incapacitating them to see or hear and follow the truth independently. Thus the Holy Quran declared : *" Fight in the way of Allah against those who fight against you, but begin not hostilities. Lo ! Allah loveth not aggressors"*[1] and, *" Fight them until persecution is no more, and religion is all for Allah."*[2]

The message of Islam thus becomes a message of peace, which none can dare ignore : *" There is no compulsion in religion. The right (direction) is henceforth distinct from error."*[3] That there are even today Christians and Jews in the Muslim world who follow their respective religions unchecked bears testimony to the irrefutable fact that Islam does not

1. 2 : 190.
2. 8 : 39.
3. 2 : 256.

approve of using force in converting men to its own viewpoint.[1].

If people accept this message of Islam and agree to follow the truth, the hostilities between them and the Muslims cease forthwith. They become part of the Muslim community and are not to be put to subjection or humiliation. They enjoy rights similar to those enjoyed by other Muslims, for no distinction is permissible between one Muslim and the other, nor any Arab had any superiority to a non-Arab except due to his piety. In the case of a people who refuse to adopt Islam as their religion but desirous to live under its protection with their own religion, Islam did not compel them to adopt its creed but gladly undertook to protect them in return for a special tax (jizyah) with the understanding that all such taxes would be paid back to them in the event of Muslims proving unable to defend them against outside aggression.[2]

---

1. The famous English writer, Mr. Arnold has upheld this claim of Islam in his book " The preaching of Islam "

2. History is full of instances such as bear upon this point, but we would mention just two out of Mr. T. W. Arnold's book " The Preaching of Islam ". (Ashraf's edition 1965) On page (61) of the book he says : " Again in the treaty made by Khalid with some towns in the neighbourhood of Hirah," he writes (Tabari, the historian): " If we protect you, then jizyah is due to us ; but if we do not, then it is not due." He goes on to say that " The Arab general, Abu Ubaydah, accordingly wrote to the governors of the conquered cities of Syria, ordering them to pay back all the jizyah that had been collected from the cities, and note to the people saying, " We give you back the money that we took from you, as we have received news that strong force is advancing against us. The agreement between us was that we should protect you, and this is not now in our power, we return you all that we took. But if we are victorious we shall consider ourselves bound to you by the old terms of our agreement."

And that despite the belief of Islam that its was a creed far superior and better to the one it had undertaken to protect. But if a people refused Islam as well as denied to pay the jizyah to the Islamic state, they were treated as real antagonists obstinately continuing in their hostilities towards Islam and turning down its offer for a peaceful agreement. They were the people who took upon themselves to arrest the spread of truth and light ruthlessly employing all their superiority in material wealth and arms. Only then and against these people it is that war is declared. But even such a war is not plunged in without a formal ultimatum or declaration as a last effort to prevent bloodshed if possible and spread peace the world over : *" And if they incline to peace incline thou also to it, and trust in Allah."* (*8 : 61*).

Such then is the story of the wars of Islam which sprang out of its wish to direct mankind to the right path if all peaceful means towards that end should prove ineffective. They were not motivated by any ambition to exploit or vanquish a people by any military commander, for they were, in a word, wars waged in the way of God. Not only this but clear injunctions and rules were also laid down for the conduct of these wars. The Holy Prophet admonishing the

Muslims said : " *Go in the name of God to fight in the way of God ; Kill him who rejects God ; fight but do not commit a perfidy, nor multilate, nor kill a child.*"[1] Also no man except he who carried arms against the Muslim army was to be killed. Nothing was to be destroyed or ruined, nor anybody's honour violated. No mischief or evil was to be encouraged, for " *Surely God does not love the mischief makers.*"

History bears witness that the Muslims upheld all these noble traditions in their wars against their enemies, including even those they had to fight against their treacherous opponents, the Crusaders. The Christians when in possession of Jerusalem committed all sorts of inequity and transgression against the Muslims living in the city. They violated their honour and recklessly put them to sword. Even the great mosque there did not escape from their transgression. But when the Muslims captured the city, they did not try to seek revenge against them although they were permitted by God to pay the transgressors back in their own coins : " *And one who attacked you, attack him in like manner, as he attacked you.*"[2] Instead they chose a course such as to this day remains unsurpassed in generosity and nobility.

---

1. Muslim, Abu Daud and Tirmizi.
2. 2 : 94.

This constituted the great fundamental distinguishing mark as to their war-aims and traditions between the Muslims and non-Muslims. Islam could very easily adopt the view that all those who insisted on their despicable idol-worship and actively fought against Truth and Light were half-human and thus fit for being held in bondage only, for how could a people not defective in their intellectual or human make-up refuse Light and Truth ? And that therefore they neither deserved respect, nor the freedom which is the privilege of human beings only.

But Islam did not adopt this course. It did not allow taking prisoners of war in servitude on the plea that they were sub-humans. They were taken slaves just because their people too treated the captured Muslims as their slaves. The problem of slavery was thus left by Islam undecided till all the belligerents should agree to a principle other than that of slavery in dealing with their prisoners of war, for, as the conditions stood, this was the only guarantee against the non-Muslims' ill-treatment of their Muslim prisoners or subjecting them to misery and humiliation without any fear of retailition.

At this place it must also be mentioned in passing that the only Quranic verse touching upon the fate of prisoners of war says that : " *And afterwards either set them free as a favour or let them ransom*

(*themselves*) *until the war lays down its weapons.*"
(47 : 4). It does not mention the enslaving of prisoners,
which would have enforced it as a permanent rule
of war. What it explicitly laid down is rather the
ransoming or setting them free as a favour, for it is
these two that the Quran prescribed as a permanent
law of war. Thus if the Muslims held the prisoners of
war in slavery it was purely an act of policy dictated
by the force of circumstances. It does not form any
intrinsic principle of the Islamic Law.

But despite this the practice generally followed in
Islam did not insist on taking prisoners of war as slaves.
If peace was restored, they were never made slaves.
The Holy Prophet set at liberty some of the Meccan
prisoners captured in the battle of Badr, in return for
a redemption, while he freed the others as a mark
of favour. Similarly he accepted the jizyah from the
Christian deputation of Najran and returned their
prisoners over to them. All these noble deeds were
meant to serve as precedents for mankind when once
it should be able to shake off the odious legacy of its
past and be ready to treat the prisoners of war
as human beings.

We may also add that the prisoners fallen in the
hands of Muslims in wars were never ill-treated,
tortured or subjected to the humiliation such as
described above. They, on the other hand, found

that if they chose, the way to freedom lay open before them, provided also that they were ready to bear the responsibilities that go with freedom. If they fulfilled these conditions they were set free, although most of them were bondsmen before falling into the hands of the. Muslims, and belonged to those slaves who were seized by Persians and Romans and packed off to fight against the Muslims.

As far as the women were concerned, Islam respected them even in their captivity even if they were taken prisoners from foreign enemy lands. No one was allowed to violate their honour or treat them merely as a part of booty captured in war. They were no longer to be treated as a common property of all with every man having free access to them to gratify his animal passions. They were henceforth to belong to their masters alone. None else could establish sexual relations with them. Moreover, they were like men, granted the right to work out their freedom through Mukatabah, besides, providing that a slave-maid would be free the moment she gave birth to a child by her master. Besides the mother, the child would also be deemed free. The treatment given them by Islam on the whole during their captivity was equally noble and generous.

Such is the story of slavery in Islam — a story which constitutes one of the brightest pages of human history. Islam never approved of slavery in principle as it strove hard with all the different means at its disposal, to eliminate slavery once for all. It tolerated its existence for the time being just because it had no other alternative, for it concerned not only Muslims but those people as well who were not under its direct control. They held the Muslims in servitude making them suffer the worst possible forms of humiliation and miseries which drove the Muslims to adopt with respect to these people a course of like-treatment, at least in treating their prisoners of war as slaves though not in their actual transactions with these slaves afterwards.

Islam could not effect the abolition of slavery so long as the world did not agree to put an end to the only source of slavery — enslavement of prisoners of war. So when that concord was achieved Islam welcomed it as it formed the unalterable fundamental principle of its polity : liberty for all, equality for all.

As to the instances of slavery, slave-traffic, seizure and sale of Muslims met with in some latter periods of Islamic history without any regular religious wars having taken place, they have no relation whatsoever to Islam. They can with no more justification, and truth be imputed to Islam than the vicious crimes and guilts that are perpetrated by some Muslim rulers in the name of Islam at the present times.

In this respect we would do well to bear the following in mind :—

(I) The governments in the latter stages of history encouraged and tolerated slavery in several ways without any genuine need. They were motivated by their lust for power and conquest, one nation or class of people holding another nation or class of people in subjection. The other forms of slavery sprang up from causes such as poverty, birth into a certain class held as inferior and the fact that a man worked as a tenant on a particular tract of land. Islam stood for the abolition of all these forms of slavery except that one and the only form of it, which, due to the unfavourable circumstances it could not effectively check. Slavery was tolerated till such time as the circumstances should grow ripe and favour its abolition.

(II) Despite the fact that in Europe slavery prevailed in so many forms without any genuine need, the Europeans in fact did never abolish it even when they at last condescended to ban it. The European writers themselves confess that in fact slavery in Europe came to an end only when due to their economic difficulties, lack of will to exert themselves and their incapacity to work, the slaves became more of an economic liability than an asset to their masters. The masters had to spend far larger amounts of money on the sustenance and supervision of their slaves than the profits they got back as a result of their exertion. It was thus a purely economic factor — just a matter of profit and loss — that helped in bringing about the liberation of these European slaves and as such it bears no analogy to that lofty ideal that respected every man for his humanity and which inspired by that lofty concept of humanity restored to the slave his freedom. The freedom thus won by the slave in Europe sinks into insignificance when viewed in the context of those successive revolutions that broke out there as a result of the restlessness among slaves and which in the end made it possible for their masters to hold them any longer in subjection.

All these series of revolutions could not, however, help the European slaves in winning back their liberty. They were rather as a result of these revolutions bound all the more securely, for henceforth they were held in serfhood bound to the soil they tilled and changed masters on the sale or transfer of land. He could not leave the soil which if he did, he was declared a fugitive by law, bound in chains, cauterized with fire and returned to his master. This form of slavery continued to exist in Europe till it was finally swept away by the French Revolution in the eighteenth century that is, some eleven hundred years after Islam had already enunciated the principle of emancipation.

We should not be taken in by beautiful names. The French Revolution in Europe and Lincoln in America abolished slavery along with the understanding among the peoples the world over to suppress it in all its forms but all these were mere names, beautiful ones of course, for, has slavery been abolished in reality? Isn't tyranny still strutting all the world over in different guises ? What is called that which the French did in Algeria ? In what other terms can we describe the black crimes of the Americans towards the negroes there ? and the felonies of the English against the coloured people of South Africa ?

Is not slavery in effect the subjection of a nation to another and the deprivation of a class of people from the rights enjoyed by other men like themselves ? It means just that and nothing else. Why should we not then call a spade a spade ? Why misname these different forms of slavery as liberty, fraternity, and equality ? for, surely the surface decoration is of little value where the crimes perpetrated underneath are of the most monstrous and hideous nature yet witnessed by mankind during their long career on earth.

Islam was very frank and explicit on what it stood for and advocated. It told the people in a straightforward manner, in clear and unequivocal terms as to what it thought of slavery, that such and such was the real cause of it, this the way out of it to freedom ; and that the way to its outright abolition .... the way that was for the time being not checked due to the disagreement among the peoples of the world as to the treatment of their prisoners of war.

But the meretricious civilization of modern times is neither so frank nor straightforward with regard to its real aims and methods. It excels in one thing only : in painting its exterior in the brightest of colours, elegant outwardly but dark and gloomy from within. It killed hundreds of thousands of people in Tunis, Algeria and Morocco just because they demanded their freedom and human dignity ; freedom to live in their respective homelands without any intrusion from abroad ; the freedom to speak their own tongue, to follow their creed and religion, and to have a free homeland and a direct share in determining their political and economic relations with the rest of the world. They killed these innocent people, hauled them into loathsome dungeons without food or water, violated their honour, raped their women folk ... killed them and ripped up their bellies wagering if the child they carried was a male or a female. These monstrous crimes are committed, but the twentieth century hypocritical civilization describes them as the propagation of the principles of liberty, fraternity and equality whereas Islam's voluntary, ideal, respectful and generous treatment of slaves thirteen centuries ago, and its declaration that slavery was not a permanent condition of life but only a temporary one, this is called backwardness, reactionarism and barbarism!

Similarly this hypocritical civilization finds nothing shocking if the Americans put on their hotels and public places the notices announcing : " For the Whites only "; " The Black and Dogs not allowed "; and when a crowd of " civilized " white Americans mercilessly lynch a coloured man throwing him on the ground and kicking him around with their boots till he is dead, for he despite being coloured had dared succumb to the temptation of having relations with a white American girl, with the initiative however, coming from her and not from him, while during all this the policemen stand around passively and do nothing to prevent them or save one of their compatriots united to them through common bonds of language, religion as well as humanity. They perpetrate all these monstrous crimes and still they remain as " civilized " as ever, and their nation is looked upon as a pinnacle of modern civilization and progress ! ! !

As against this we see that when a parsee slave threatened Omar with assassination Omar did not say anything to the slave although he understood what the threat implied. The slave was neither imprisoned, nor banished from the country, nor did Omar order his execution on the plea that he belonged to a sub-human species who out of sheer prejudice and insolence insisted on worshipping falsehood even after he had with his own eyes seen the truth and the light. How vulgar of him and how contemptuous his attitude towards the slave as a man when he on hearing the threat said instead : " The slave has threatened me." and then went his way without in anyway curtailing his freedom. He was charged with the assassination of the caliph only after he did actually commit the heinous crime

On the other hand we see that the coloured people of Africa are oppressed, killed or as the English papers put it, are hunted down ; and their human rights withheld from them as they have dared realize their human dignity and so demand of the English people their freedom. This is the English justice at its highest and the human civilization at its bes ! ! And these precisely are the " sublime " and " glorious " moral principles on the basis of which Europe claims precedence and dominance over the whole of the world. But so far as Islam is concerned it is extremely barbarous and frivolous, for adopting the course of a like-treatment towards its enemies, it allowed the enslaving of prisoners of war temporarily without, however, approving of slavery in principle. It is also very backward for it never allowed ' man-hunting,' nor did it indulge in the killing of men because of their having a black skin. Far from that its reactionarism advanced to such an extent that it declared : " Hear and obey even if the one appointed over you be a negro slave with a raisin-like head."

As far as women slaves were concerned they constituted a quite different problem.

Islam made it lawful for a master to have a number of slave women captured in wars and enjoined that he alone may have sexual relations with them and that he might, if he wished, marry anyone of them. Europe abhors this law but at the same time gladly allows that most odious form of animalism according to which a man may have illicit relations with any girl coming across him on his way to gratify his animal passions without any consideration whatsoever to any law or human dignity. The guilt of Islam in reality is that it did not countenance adultery. That is why the Europeans seem so wroth with it.

The women captured in wars, were among other nations forced to lead a shameful and vile life of prostitution, for they had none to take care of or look after them and as their masters' sense of honour was seldom injured by their pursuing such a wicked course of life. Far from it, the masters would often rather force them to it for their own material gains. But Islam, " *the reactionary and backward Islam,* " never countenanced adultery ; it rather made efforts to keep society clean of this hideous moral taint. Therefore, it enjoined that these slave women would belong to their masters only ; they were to provide for their maintenance, feed and safeguard them from falling a prey to such a depravation gratifying their sexual needs along with satisfying their own in a clean respectable manner.

But the " conscientious" Europe cannot bring itself to countenance this animalism. That is why it approves of adultery extending it all possible support and protection of law and then not content with that spreads its cult throughout the world wherever its imperialistic designs would lead it. The names have changed but the reality behind them remains unchanged : The woman is as slave to the lust of men as ever she was, for is a modern prostitute despite all her much publicized freedom, really free to reject her customers — the customers who have no interest in her save as a means to achieve the gratification of their own animal urge ? Is she really a free woman ? There is nothing common in this filthy abominable trade of human bodies and that clean and spiritual bond that ties a maid to her master in Islam.

As against Islam modern civilization lacks definiteness and clarity of vision. It does for instance recognize that prostitution is an institution of slavery, but still insists on its continuance on the plea that it is a " social necessity ".

And why do Europeans consider prostitution a " social necessity " ?

Prostitution has come to stay as a social necessity in European civilization because a " civilized " European does not want to burden himself by supporting anyone, a wife or children. He wants to have pleasure without the responsibilities that it generally carries with it. Therefore what he seeks is a woman, no matter who she is, or what she thinks of him or he of her, for the gratification of his sexual instinct. He wants her body and nothing else. As such he is far from being attached to any particular woman, for he may satisfy his animal passion with any woman walking in the street.

This is the social necessity on the basis of which slavery of women in the modern epoch is justified. However, it is no more than a mere bluff, for it ceases to exist the moment the European man should get rid of his vanity and animal passions and agree to ascend to a higher plane of humanity.

It may also be mentioned here that the civilized western governments which at last prohibited prostitution did not act so out of any respect for the human status of a prostitute as such, nor did it in any way manifest their moral, psychological and spiritual elevation rendering them immune to this crime. It rather sprang out of the fact that these prostitutes had lost all their usefulness, their place having been taken by the common sybaritic society girls. The crime was no longer regarded as a crime. And the governments just did not feel any need to interfere with the freedom of its citizens.

But still the Europeans have the audacity to blame Islam for its solution of the problem of captive women thirteen hundred years ago declaring that it was just a temporary arrangement and was not meant to perpetuate for ever and notwithstanding the fact that the system Islam stood for was far more superior and cleaner to that represented by their twentieth century modern civilization, the natural and the most perfect one, according to them that none may dare disown or even think of changing, it being the pinnacle of human civilization and as such destined to last for ever.

We must not be taken in by the ostensible freedom with which these sybaritic modern society girls surrender themselves to others and think that they are free, for we know that there has always been a group of slaves who were glad to surrender their freedom and willingly accept their former state of servitude. But such readiness on the part of certain slavish individuals to forego their free human status is no justification to perpetuate their servitude according to Islam as well as any other religion or philosophy of life. This phenomenon is however a very sad reflection on the system of life that creates economic, social, political, philosophical and spiritual conditions under which people willingly prefer servitude to freedom. That is what European civilization has in fact accomplished. It encourages adultery and moral corruption be it in the form of traditional prostitution or in the presence of the sybarite society girls who willingly surrender themselves to men.

This in short is the story of slavery in Europe right up to this twentieth century : slavery of men, women , of whole nations and classes. It was a slavery that sprang up from various new sources and causes ; a slavery that was sustained without any real and genuine social need such as thirteen hundred years ago forced Islam to tolerate one and an inevitable form of it. It was founded in the vileness of European civilization and its innate inhuman character.

We may add a word about slavery under which the peoples of the communist countries are groaning. The government is the only master in these countries, all the other people are just slaves to it ever ready to obey orders. Men and women do not even have the freedom to choose their job or the place they would like to work in. They are no more than slaves. A similar situation prevails in the capitalist countries of the West where big capitalists are the virtual masters who wield real power. The working classes are helpless and completely dependent upon them.

The reader may come across the votaries and supporters of one or the other of these systems but he may never be taken in by their loud professions if he would but keep in mind all that we have briefly sketched above. From this he can easily judge for himself if both these systems — capitalism and communism — are any thing more than the continuance of all those centuries old forms of slavery that have been imposed on people in the name of civilization and social development. He can also see whether mankind during the last fourteen centuries has continually moved ahead on the path of progress and glory by ignoring the guidance of Islam or has it instead been steadily sinking low going down and down showing thereby how desperately it stands in need of the guidance of Islam to help it get out of the darkness it has long since been plunged in.

ISLAM AND FEUDALISM

Recently when I heard that a student wrote a thesis wherein he " proved " that Islam was a feudalistic system and received his Master's Degree, I was deeply surprised. The performance of both the student as well as the professors awarding him the degree was equally mystifying. But the student might well be excused on the plea that he was either ignorant of what he was writing about or did so out of ill-will towards Islam, but what about the learned teachers ? How are we to account for their conduct ? their knowledge of the socio-economic system of Islam, and their understanding of history ?

But I no longer wondered as I remembered who these learned teachers were. Weren't they the members of a community enticed by the foreign exploiters and fashioned after an intellectual pattern serviceable to them ? Aren't they the people in whom Mr. Dunlop[1] was particularly interested ? They were sent abroad ostensibly to aquire knowledge but in fact it was just a part of a conspiracy to turn them complete strangers to their own culture and civilization ; to make them look down upon their religion, their

---

I.   Dunlop was the British official entrusted by British Coloniolist authorities to plan and supervise educational policy in Egypt.

own selves, their history, their faith and instead follow in the footsteps of their western teachers. No wonder then that they allowed such a monstrous perversion of history and truth !

Let us however see what the word feudalism means in fact and what are its characteristics. For this purpose we reproduce below extracts of a book, " Communism " by Dr. Rashid-al-Barawy, that has recently been published in Europe. Speaking about feudalism, the author says that : " Feudalism is a way of production the distinguishing mark of it being the existence of a perpetual system of serfdom. It is a system wherein the landlord or his representative is entitled to receive a fixed share of production and enjoys certain specific economic rights, carrying with them the privilege to make their tenants serve them or instead thereof receive payments from them in cash or kind. As an explanation of this, we may say that feudal society is divided into two classes of people : (1) the owners of feudal lands, and (2) the tenants, who may again vary in their grades, farmers, agricultural workers, and slaves, the number of some of them dwindling off more rapidly than that of others. It is the farmers, the direct producers, however, who enjoy the right to possess land and have a share in produce that is so necessary for them to support their families and themselves, besides the right to build farm-houses on the tillage. Against these benefits they are required to serve the landlord every week by rendering free services in his fields working with their own cattle and instruments, along with performing for him a number of other services at the time of harvesting and reaping, and offering him on the occasion of festivals whatever gifts and presents they can. They are also expected to get their food-grains and grapes milled and pressed in his flour mills and pressing machines.

The landlord also exercises full executive and judicial powers over his tenants living within the bounds of his feudal lands.

"The real producer in feudalism did not enjoy freedom in the sense we know at present ; he did not own the land, nor could he sell, inherit or give it as a free gift to others. He was compelled to a forced labour in the lands of his master even at the expense of his own material gains or considerations thereof. Moreover as a mark of his obedience to the master he had to pay him taxes that were unlimited in amount as well as extent. With the land he too changed masters passing from one to the other, for he did not have the right to shift of his own free will from one fief to another in search of work or even join the service of still another master. As such the feudal villein forms the connecting link between the slaves of olden times and the free tenants of the modern times.

" It was the master who fixed the extent of the land to be given by him to the peasant. He also decided about the services that he expected his tenants to render him without being under any obligation to have a consideration for the rights of the other land owners or the needs of the peasants while making such momentous decisions."

The writer goes on to say that : " In the thirteenth century there ensued the great illegal migration movement that finally ended with the emergence of agricultural workers. This movement known as " the running away of peasants ", caused the landowners to claim back their fugitive tenants. They among themselves agreed that every land-owner would be fully authorised to capture all the workers happening to transgress into his feudal domain. But as the phenomenon—the running away of the peasants—was fast becoming a common feature of the times, the land-owners were forced to depend on and consequently engage more and more of hired labour for the tilling of their lands. Their mutual agreements gradually lost all significance which meant a steady decrease in their co-operation. From this proceeded still another inevitable result : wages to the workers were paid in cash in place of exacting forced labour out of them without any payment.

" Many of the peasants gradually prospered as against the needs of the nobility and land-owners that were greatly multiplied and hence became a great burden on them economically. The circumstances favoured the peasants and they bought off their freedom. This continued till the fourteenth century when the freedom of the agricultural workers was at last recognized as such by all. However, the important change that came over the times was that the basis on which the whole feudal structure rested was beginning to give way ; the following centuries witnessed its complete abolition. [1] "

These are the characteristics of feudalism, we have reproduced these extracts above in detail as we want that we should become clear-headed about feudalism and its characteristics and not confuse them with other seemingly similar manifestations. Bearing all these characteristics of a feudalistic society in mind may we ask : when and where was such feudalism ever witnessed in the history of Islam ?

Perhaps the outward semblance that has proved a stumbling block for many a research worker or has given

---

I.   An-Nizam-ul-Ishtiraki " Communism " pp. 22-23.

the opportunists an excuse to cast aspersions against Islam, is the fact that in the beginning, the Islamic society for the time being consisted of two classes of people : the land-owners and the peasants who worked in their lands. But this was nothing more than a mere outward semblance. It in no wise justifies the confusion of Islam with feudalism. In order to facilitate a comparison between Islam and feudalism we may sum up the basic characteristics of feudalism as follows :—

(1) A perpetual serfdom,

(2) The duties which the peasant discharged to-wards his master, consisted of :

(a) a whole day's free and forced labour in the lands of his feudal lord once a week ;

(b) free and forced services rendered by him to his master in special seasons of harvesting, etc.

(c) presenting gifts on religious and other similar occasions of festivities, notwithstanding his poverty or the opulance of the recipient rich land-lord ;

(d) an obligation to get his food grains milled in the mills of the land-lord. (we pass over his obligation to get his grapes pressed by his feudal lord as wine is prohibited in Islam).

(3)   The right of the landlord to decide as his whims or desires might dictate as to the extent of the land to be held by the peasant, the services required of him and the taxes to be paid by him ;

(4)   The exercise of all judicial-cum-executive powers by the landlord not in accordance with a fixed law of the land but according to his own whims and desires ;

(5)   The obligation of the peasants to buy off their freedom with cash payments when in the end feudalism gave way and a process of its degeneration set in.

Let the readers first look at these and then glance over the whole history of Islam to find similar characteristics therein. They will surely be disappointed for Islam has nothing to do with them.

There is no serfdom in Islam as it recognizes no other form of servitude save that of slavery, the causes and conditions whereof and the means of freedom from which we have already dealt with in the preceding chapter. Islam admits of no bondage arising out of a tenant's being bound to the soil. The only slaves that we know of in Islam were those captured in wars which is quite sufficient to prove that in the early Islamic society the number of slaves was far less in comparison with the total number of its free citizens. They worked on the soil of their masters till they were freed voluntarily or they themselves took the initiative and demanded a writing of (Mukatabah) their freedom of their masters. But there exists no such parallel in the history of the European feudalism as it primarily aimed at the subjection of the peasants as well as the agricultural workers rather than encourage them to demand freedom. That is why the peasants in Europe were looked upon as serfs bound to and transferable with the land from one master to another. As such they could neither leave the soil they worked on, nor free themselves from the obligations devolving upon them towards their landlords.

Islam is not at all familiar with this type of serfdom or villeins as it is in principle opposed to all forms of servitude save that rendered by man unto his God, the Creator of all life. There is no provision in it for the subjection of some creatures to other creatures like them. Whenever such an abnormal state-subjection of some men to others is found due to certain external causes without any initiative from Islam, it is always a temporary or a transitional phenomenon, which it strives to do away with all the possible resources at its disposal, encouraging the slaves to earn their freedom besides holding the state responsible to render to them all possible help towards that end.

In economics too Islam does not recognize any bondage of man to other men like him. The system of slavery to which we have alluded above is an exception as there was no other economical alternative before Islam at the time. Islam tolerated it till the slaves were freed spiritually and till the time they were able to shoulder their responsibilities as free members of the community, whereupon Islam actively helped them in winning back their lost freedom.

Islam bases its economic structure on freedom of action coupled with a relationship of a complete co-operation and exchange of mutual services among all individuals. The Islamic Government as such acts as a guardian and custodian of all such people as happen to lag behind in the struggle of life for some reason and are denied all amenities of a decent living. Thus with all the resources of the state at his backing in an Islamic community, no man needs let himself become a bondsman to the land-owners. Islam provides for all his basic needs without degrading him or making him lose his independence, self-respect or honour.

Thus both spiritually and economically Islam is opposed to feudalism. It brought to men freedom from feudalism even before they were caught up in the shackles of serfdom.

So far as the obligations of the peasant towards his feudal lords are concerned there is no evidence whatever of their existence in the whole range of

Islamic history. It is quite free of such nonsense. In this respect Islam stands quite unique. In case a peasant is found guilty of some crime it allows the owner of the land to discard him and give away the land to another one. But this is not to encourage oppression ; it is rather a step towards the eradication of serfdom. Islam aims at the establishment of a free relationship between the landlord and the tenant.

The only relationship that Islam recognizes as lawful between the peasant and the landlord is either that of contract or that based on tenancy. In the former case the peasant is required to pay to the landlord a fixed amount as the rent of the land proportionate to its produce and after that he remains quite free in his cultivation, expenditure as well as in the acquiring of all the produce of the land for his own personal consumption. If he happens to be a tenant he will share the produce of the land at the end of every year with the landlord. In such a case all the expenses are borne by the landlord; the peasant provides the labour only. In both of these cases there is no place for forced labour, dictatorial privileges or any other obligation incumbent on the peasant to serve his master without getting any thing in return. Both parties rather enjoy full equality in freedom, in their rights as well as duties with a reciprocity of mutual give-and-take relationship. The peasant is, in the first place, quite free to choose the land he would like to hire or the landlord he would prefer to work with as a tenant. Secondly, he is on a par with the landlord and enjoys as much freedom to decide or agree to the amount for the contract to be paid by him to the landlord. If he does not find the bargain profitable he is free to back out of it and not agree to the contract, the landlord having no power or right to take him to task for that. As a tenant the peasant enjoys as much legal privileges as his landlord. They divide the profit thereof equally between themselves.

Besides this we also find that contrary to what happened in the history of European feudalism, the practice commonly prevalent in Islam was quite different. It was the rich landlord and not the poor peasant who gave presents and bestowed bountiful gifts upon his tenants on the occasions of Eid and other festivals. This is specially true about the month of Ramadhan, a month of great importance and religious significance in Islam. During this month friends and relations paid visits to each other and were entertained with feasts along with bestowing bountiful gifts upon the poor and needy ones of their community. It means in other words that the rich and well-to-do people were wont to spend their riches on others rather than exact costly gifts from the poor people as was the custom in the " civilized " Europe.

From this it is clear that the duties that the peasants were encumbered with in feudalism and which degenerated into forced labour have no place in the Islamic system of life. It establishes rather a free relationship between the landowner and peasants with a reciprocal respect and perfect equality. As regards the duties discharged by the feudal lords in Europe towards their tenants as a recompense for their unjustifiable forced labour and abject slavery to them in the form of defending them from others and safeguarding their rights, in Islamic society the rich people discharged voluntarily similar duties with regard to their tenants without expecting anything from them in return. In rendering these services towards their fellowmen they sought nothing save God's pleasure. This is what distinguishes a system of life based on a lofty creed and the one devoid of it. In the one the social services rendered by a man towards others assume the character of a worship whereby he is brought closer to his God, whereas in the other they are nothing more than a commercial enterprise each party striving hard to get hold of the lion's share and anxious to yield to the other nothing but that which is beyond its power to hold longer, with the result that in the end the most powerful party rather than the one rightfully deserving emerges victorious and makes away with all the profits.

The third characteristic of feudalism, that is, the right of the feudal lord to decide as to the extent of the land to be given to the tenant and prescribe the duties to be charged by and expected of him, is a thing peculiar to the European concept of lordship and serfdom only. Such concept had never existed in the history of Islam which does not recognize the over-lordship of the feudal lord or the serfhood of the peasant to him. The only factor which does restrict the choice of a peasant with regard to his acquiring a lease of land in Islam is his own free will and financial potentiality. The lessor enjoys no privileges against this save that of claiming the agreed upon rent of the land from the peasant. Similarly in tenancy the extent of the land to be farmed by a tenant is deter-mined by his own physical ability or the number of the helping hands (consisting of his sons generally) he can get hold of. The duties imposed on him in tenancy are no more than what the rehabilitation of the land acquired by him may necessitate. The land in such a case is considered as a common property of the peasant and the land owner till it brings forth its produce. As to the land of the landlord other than that held by the tenant in tenancy, the tenant is not supposed to have any thing to do with that, nor is he under any obligation to work therein whatever the form or nature of such a work or service might be.

The most striking point of difference between Islam and feudalism however, is the judicial-cum-executive prerogative enjoyed by the landlord in feudalism. He alone in feudalism controls and regulates all social and political life within the bounds of his fiefs. Islam is diametrically opposed to such a prerogative as it aims at the abolition, rather than its retention in the world of human relationships.

The European nations did not possess any law of the land in the real sense of the word with regard to the above mentioned landlord-tenant relationship. The Roman Law which later on formed the basis of all latter European legislation conferred upon the feudal lords the right to become virtual dictators in their respective areas, make laws for the people, hold judicial powers among them, and enforce their decisions as they might think fit. Thus they held in their persons legislative, judicial and executive powers all in one and at the same time. Each one of them formed a government within a government. The government did not interfere with the internal affairs of the feudal monarchies so long as they continued to carry out their financial and military obligations towards it at the hour of the need.

Nothing of the sort is to be found in Islam. It had its own central government with its own law of the land which it strove to enforce in the lives of all those living within its boundaries. Judges were appointed to enforce the law of the land in all parts of the country. All were made equal before law. None enjoyed any priority over others. The individual was called to account only when he committed a mistake or acted wrongly. Later on when contrary to the teachings of Islam, the government degenerated into a hereditary monarchy it still retained some Islamic characteristics. Thus for instance, the government continued exercising a supervisory authority over all the different peoples and individuals that lived within its sphere of influence. The law of the land was one and the same for all people living within its vast territories. The only exception appears to be differences of the jurists among themselves on certain legal points, which is no more than what is met with in almost all the systems of law found on the face of the earth. It was this rule of the law that provided a safeguard for the peasants against the oppression of the feudal lords as well as their greed, lust or whim. They were ruled in accordance with the divine law rather than the whims and wishes of the feudal lords. It held not only the landlords and the tenants as equals as both of them were now made free men but also treated all men alike and in the same manner.

Of course there are found certain unfortunate incidents in the history of Muslims as well wherein we see that judges gave judgement contrary to their own conscience as well as in contravention of the spirit of the law in order to win favour with the feudal lords or the rulers, but these incidents were no more than certain stray instances. They are merely exceptions, as is shown by the historical facts to the veracity of which even the European scholars bear witness. As against these few stray cases of injustice there are a great many instances in Islamic history which show that judges gave judgement in favour of extremely poor men against not only landlords, governors or ministers but even against the caliph himself — the caliph who wielded absolute authority and power. But inspite of this neither any judge was dismissed from his post, nor did the ruler seek any revenge against him.

Similarly there is not any escape movement of the peasants met with in the Islamic history as was witnessed in Europe. This was so because the peasants enjoyed not only the rights to move freely from one farm to the other but also from one country to another within the boundaries of the vast Islamic Empire. Nothing prevented them from shifting from place to place except their own fondness for or attachment to a particular tract of land as was, for instance, the case with the Egyptian farmers. The peasants in other parts of the Islamic world, however, fully availed themselves of this freedom of movement as they did not happen to be so attached to their particular areas as their Egyptian counterparts were and as no obstacles were hurled in their way to prevent their movement such as blocked the way in the case of the European peasants in the form of serfdom and the various obligations they were encumbered upon with.

The peasants in the history of the European feudalism towards its final phase had to buy off their freedom. This too has no parallel in the history of the Islamic peoples, for the simple reason that among them the peasants enjoyed as much freedom as any other section of the community did. They as such had no need to buy off the freedom they already possessed.

Moreover it may also be added that in the Islamic world a large number of small states existed throughout its history. These estates provided livelihood to their possessors, helped them carry out various kinds of sea or land trade and support the various industrial crafts. But in Europe all of these were completely swept away by the upsurge of feudalism. It was then that a dark night of spiritual ignorance and intellectual darkness settled on Europe. It was shown light by Islam, first when it came into contact with the Islamic world during the crusades, and again, when the two encountered with each other in Spain. These encounters set Europe onto the path to the Renaisance and so Europe gradually climbed out of that dark night of intellectual and spiritual stagnation.

Thus we find that feudalism as such did never exist in the world of Islam so long as Islam remained dominant in the Muslim lands, as its spiritual, economic system as well as its basic creed, principles and laws are all opposed to feudalism. Not only this but it also does away with all the causes conducive to its growth. Whatever semblance of feudalism was witnessed during the Ommeyed and Abasside periods was limited in its sphere besides the fact that it never flourished so as to become a common feature of the social life of the Muslims.

Of course we do find feudalism in the Islamic countries in the modern history towards the end of the Ottoman Empire, when headsprings of Islamic faith had dried up in the hearts of Muslims and the political power had passed into the hands of those who knew nothing as regards Islam save its name. The picture became all the more dark when the godless, materialistic and aggressive European civilization marched in triumph against the Islamic world. It staged military occupations, destroyed all spiritual values and put an end to the spirit of co-operation, replacing these with the most hideous forms of capitalistic exploitation, and a life-long misery to the poor. This feudalistic system imported as it was from Europe still continues to linger on in some of the Muslim lands with all those features that characterised its parent — the European feudalism. It is quite clear that Islam owes no apology for the presence of it in the contemporary Islamic world, nor is it in any way responsible for its emergence or existence. It could be held responsible only if it were a ruling power in the Muslim lands. Some Muslim rulers are at present ruling their peoples in accordance with the constitutions and laws imported from various European countries rather than according to the Islamic laws. They remain the most faithful followers of their western masters, that were ever witnessed on the face of the earth.

From the above discussion certain facts stand out clearly that have become a centre of the ideological conflict raging in the modern world. Of these the following facts may be pointed out :—

(1) It is not the factor of ownership as such that inexorably paves the way for the growth of feudalism with human will having no part in its enhancement. It is rather the manner of possessing and the nature of relationship between the owners of the land and those who have no land in their possession that favours its growth. That is why ownership was there in the Islamic world and yet feudalism did not exist because the ideology of Islam as well as its various applications to practical life establish between the individuals such relationships as do not favour the growth of feudalism.

(2) If Europe was condemned to feudalism it was not because feudalism is an essential stage of evolution on the path of evolution that can never be bypassed by mankind even if it should desire to. Europe suffered from it rather because of the fact that it did not possess any system or creed such as

might have regulated human relationships and offered a sound intellectual guidance. Had there been present such a creed and ideology as was the case with the world of Islam, to guide and organize their socio-economic relationships, no feudalism could ever have sprung up or flourished in Europe .

(3) The different stages of economic evolution — first communist society, slavery, feudalism, capitalism and then the final communist society — which the dialectical materialists describe as a common phenomenon in the history of mankind, really have no existence whatsoever outside the European history. These stages were never passed through by any people outside Europe. The world of Islam never in its whole history passed through the stage of feudalism ; it has never also as such till now come to the stage of communism, nor will it ever reach that stage.

ISLAM AND CAPITALISM

Capitalism did not originate in the Islamic world as it came into being only after the invention of the machine — which took place by chance in Europe.

Capitalism was imported into the Islamic world at a time when it was under European domination. Together with the wave of development, it spread into the Islamic world which suffered from poverty, ignorance, illness and backwardness. This made some people think that Islam approves of capitalism, with both its evils and merits. They also claim that there are no provisions in the Islamic law or regulations such as might be in conflict with capitalism. They argue that as Islam permitted individual ownership it must likewise permit capitalism.

In answer to this accusation it might suffice to point out that capitalism cannot prosper or grow without usury and monopoly both of which were prohibited by Islam about one thousand years before the existence of capitalism.

But let us tackle the question at some greater length. If the invention of the machine had taken place in the Islamic world, how would Islam have faced the economic development resulting from such invention ? How would Islamic legislations and laws have organised work and production ?

There is concensus of opinion among economists — including those who are opposed to capitalism i.e. Karl Marx — that capitalism at the start brought about great progress and rendered considerable services to humanity. Production was increased, means of communications were improved and national resources were exploited at a larger scale. The standard of living among the working classes became higher than when they were mostly or completely dependent on agriculture.

But such a glorious picture did not last long because the natural development of capitalism, as they say, led to the amassing of wealth in the hands of capitalist owners and to a relative diminution of the properties owned by the working classes. This enabled the capitalist owners to use workmen — the real producers in communist eyes—in considerably stepping up the production of various commodities but the wages paid to workmen were too low to ensure decent life, because the employers took all the profits and spent them leading a life of luxury and corruption.

Besides this the scanty wages paid to workmen did not enable them to consume all the production of capitalist countries. This led to the accumulation of surplus production. As a result of this the capitalist countries began to look for new markets for their surplus production, which in turn gave rise to colonialism with all its incessant conflicts among different nations over markets and raw material resources. Destructive wars were the inevitable outcome of all this.

Moreover, the capitalist system is always exposed to periodic crises resulting from depression caused by low wages and the scantiness of world consumption in relation to increasing production.

Some propagandists of materialism refer all the problems of the capitalist system to the nature of capital itself rather than to any ill-will or desire for exploitation on the part of the capitalists. Such naive and strange reasoning means that man with all his emotions and thoughts is but a helpless creature in the face of the power of economy.

There is no doubt that Islam would have encouraged the good and progressive achievements that were brought about by capitalism in its early stage. But Islam would not have left capitalism without a legislation to organise it and to preclude any exploitation which might result from ill-will on the part of the employers or from the very nature of capital. The Islamic principle which was laid in this respect entitles the workmen to share the profit with their employers. Some Maliki jurisprudents went so far as to give to the employee an equal share in the profit. The employer provides all capital and the workman does the work ; the two efforts are equal and accordingly they are entitled to an equal share in the profit.

The above mentioned principle illustrates Islam's great concern with the establishment of justice. Such concern for the establishment of justice was voluntarily introduced by Islam. It was not forced thereon by any economic exigency nor was it the result of the struggle among classes which is regarded by the propagandists of certain economic doctrines as the sole effective factor in the development of economic relations.

In the beginning industry consisted of simple manual work involving a small number of workmen who worked in simple workshops. The above mentioned principle would have organised the relation between work and capital on an equitable basis such as Europe had never had.

Economists say that the development of capitalism from its early benevolent phase to its present morbidly evil phase was accompanied by its increasing dependence on national loans. This led to the creation of banks which carried on financial operations, and advanced loans in return for some interest. Without that such loans as well as the majority of banking operations are based on usury which is expressly prohibited by Islam.

On the other hand, tough competition which is another feature of capitalism leads to the destruction of minor companies or to their merger into major ones. This encourages monopoly which is also prohibited by Islam, as is borne out by some sayings of the Prophet. He said : " *He that monopolises is a wrong doer.*" Because Islam prohibited usury and monopoly it would have been impossible for capitalism to develop under Islam into its present evil stage which involves exploitation, colonialism and war.

What would have been the fate of industry if it had originated under Islamic rule ?

Surely Islam would not have restricted industry to minor workshops whose profit is shared by the employer and the workman. Production would have rather grown but the relationship between the employer and workmen would have developed on different lines from those outlining the development of the employer-employee relations in Europe in the nineteenth and twentieth centuries. It would have developed in accordance with the basic principles of Islam such as the above mentioned principle which provides for an equal division of profit between the workmen and their employer.

By so doing Islam would have avoided resorting to usury or monopoly and would have precluded the injustice to which workmen are subjected under capitalism when they are exploited and left to suffer poverty and humiliation.

It would be foolish to suggest that Islam could not have established such justice without first passing through hard ordeals, class conflicts and economic pressures which would ultimately lead to the amendment of its legislations. It is proved beyond all doubt that Islam had been ahead of all nations in dealing with the questions of slavery, feudalism and early capitalism. In so doing Islam was not acting under any outside pressure whatsoever. It was rather acting voluntarily and in accordance with its own conception of eternal equity and justice scoffed at by the communist writers. On the other hand it is a fact that Russia, a model communist state, itself passed directly from feudalism to communism without passing through the intermediary stage of capitalism. In this way Russia — which adopted the doctrine of Karl Marx — practically puts to the lie Marx's theory regarding the phases of development which, he says, every state has to experience.

As to colonialism, wars and exploitation of peoples it should be pointed out that Islam is firmly opposed to all these as well as to all the other universal evils engendered by capitalism. It is not one of the principles of Islam to colonise other peoples or to wage any war against others for the purposes of exploitation. The only war approved by Islam is that which is waged against aggression or is meant to spread the word of God where its peaceful dissemination is rendered impossible by the force of arms.

The communists and their like allege that colonialism is an inevitable phase in human development. They add that colonialism could not have been averted by any doctrines or moral principles since it was essentially an economic phenomenon resulting from a surplus in the production of industrialised countries and the need for foreign outlets for marketing such surplus.

Needless to say, Islam does not recognize such nonsense about the inevitability of colonialism. Besides, the communists themselves say or profess that Russia will solve the problem of surplus production by reducing both working hours and workmen's role in production. The solution which communism professes to have found may be used by other systems as well.

History bears witness that colonialism has been an ancient human propensity. It did not originate with capitalism ; although capitalism with its modern weapons of destruction rendered it more ferocious. As to the exploitation of the vanquished, Roman colonialists were more ruthless and monstrous than their modern counterparts.

History furnishes us with best evidence to the effect that Islam has been the cleanest of all systems as far as war is concerned. Islamic wars have always been free from exploitation as well as subjection of others. Therefore, if the industrial revolution had taken place in Islamic countries, Islam would have solved the problem of surplus production without resorting to war or colonisation. Besides, it may be said that the problem of surplus production is an outcome of the capitalist system in its present form only. In other words if the basic principles of capitalism are changed, the problem would not exist.

As against this the ruler in the Islamic state shall not remain helplessly indifferent towards the problem of the accumulation of wealth in the hands of a few people while the majority are suffering from poverty and deprivation. Such amassing of wealth is contrary to the principles of Islam which expressly prescribed that wealth should be fairly distributed among all people lest it should be confined to the rich only. The ruler in Islam is charged with the enforcement of Sharia (Islamic law) by all means at his command without any injustice or harm to anyone. In this respect, the ruler is invested with full and unlimited powers within the bounds set by God's law — the law that precludes the accumulation of wealth. We might refer in this respect to the law of inheritance which ensures that the wealth left by each generation is properly distributed. Reference should also be made to Al-zakat which prescribes that $2^1/_2 \%$ of the capital and profit should be annually earmarked for the poor. In addition, Islam explicitly prohibits the hoarding up of wealth. It likewise prohibits usury which is the basic factor in the accumulation of capital. Moreover the relationships among the members of Islamic society are based on reciprocal responsibility rather than exploitation.

It should also be added that the Holy Prophet (peace be on him) ensured for officials of the state certain rights including the basic necessities of life : " *If a person who is charged with work for us (i.e. the state) has no wife, he shall have one ; if he has no dwelling place, he shall have one, if he has no servant, he shall have one, if he has no animal, he shall have one.*"

Such guarantees are not to be confined to officials of the state only. They are the basic necessities required by every person. They can be obtained in return for work done in the service of the state or through any profession or occupation from which society may benefit. If the state ensures the basic necessities for its officials it must also ensure the same for every working individual in the state. This is evident from the fact that the Public Treasury is responsible for supporting those who are unable to work owing to old age, illness, or childhood. The Public Treasury is also responsible for providing the basic necessities to persons who cannot obtain them owing to the insufficiency of their means.

All the above mentioned facts emphasize the responsibility of the state to ensure by all means the basic necessities for workers. It is of no great importance as to by what means it is that such necessities are provided to the workers ; what really matters is the principle which guarantees that profit and loss shall be equally shared by all members of the nation. By providing such necessities for workers Islam protects them against exploitation besides ensuring a decent life for all.

Islam would not have allowed capitalism to grow into the monstrous forms which are presently prevalent in the " civilised " West. The Islamic legislations — whether originally prescribed by Sharia or newly adopted to face new developments within the framework of Sharia — would not have allowed the capitalists to exploit the working people or suck their blood. Islam would have precluded all the evils of capitalism including colonisation, war and the enslaving of people.

Islam, as usual, is not content with the mere enactment of economic rules and laws. In addition to law, Islam also makes use of moral and spiritual incentives which are satirised by the communists because they see that such values have no practical significance in Europe. But in Islam moral and spiritual values are not separated from practical considerations. Islam has a unique manner of combining and harmonising both the purification of the spirit and the organisation of the community. The individual is never left to wonder how to reconcile the ideal and the practical. Islam formulates its legislations on a moral basis so that the moral values are always in harmony with the legislation. In this way, each side supplements the other without any fear of conflict or divorcement.

Islamic morality prohibits and discourages all forms of luxury and sensuality which are inevitable results of the amassing of wealth in the hands of a few people. Along with this, Islam also prohibits being unjust to employees or underpaying them. As the amassing of wealth is an outcome of injustice to employees it invariably means that it must also be discouraged. Islam calls on people to spend their money in the way of God — even if that should lead to disposing of all one's property. It is because the rich people spend their money on themselves rather than in the way of God that the majority of the people live in poverty and deprivation.

The spiritual elevation of men brought about by Islam brings them closer to God and makes them renounce all worldly pleasures and profits in striving to attain God's pleasure and in expectation of His recompense in the other world. There is no doubt that a man who keeps his peace with God and has faith in the other world, in heaven and hell, will not rush madly for the amassing of wealth or resort to exploitation or injustice for the realization of his selfish ends.

In this way the moral and spiritual edification will pave the way for economic legislations which aim at curbing the evils of capitalism. Consequently, when such legislations are made they are sure to be complied with not because of fear of punishment but rather because people would be acting according to the dictates of their conscience.

In conclusion, it should be made clear that the monstrous capitalism which is currently prevalent in Islamic world is not a part of Islam and consequently Islam cannot be held responsible for its evils.

———◆———

ISLAM AND PRIVATE OWNERSHIP

Is private ownership a natural propensity ?

Communists and their likes insist that it is not. They claim that there was no private property in the earliest societies where the " first communism " prevailed. All things, they say, were public property shared by all people who were guided by a spirit of affection, cooperation and brotherhood. They sadly regret that such " an angelic era " did not last because the discovery of agriculture involved disputes over the cultivated land and the means of production. This inevitably led to war. The communists allege that humanity can put an end to this dreadful evil only by returning once more to " the first communism " where no one had a property of one's own and all production was equally shared by all people. They believe that this is the only way to restore peace, affection and harmony to the world.

On the other hand, psychologists and sociologists do not agree upon a clear distinction between natural and acquired human emotions, concepts and manners. Likewise they differ regarding private ownership. Some psychologists and sociologists maintain that private ownership is a natural propensity born with man regardless of the conditions of his environment. Others believe that it is acquired through man's environment. A child, they say, refuses to part with any of his toys either because they are too few or because he fears that another child may take them. When there is just one toy for ten children, quarrel is sure to break out, but, they say, where there are ten toys for ten children every one will have a toy of his own and there will be no conflict.

Our answer to the arguments put forward by communist and other psychologists and sociologists is as follows :—

1. No scientist has been able to prove beyond all doubt that private ownership is not the outcome of a natural instinct. All that the leftists could say in this regard is that there is no conclusive evidence available that it is the outcome of a natural instinct. But that is another question.

2. The example — about children and their toys — which the communists give in support of their stand cannot lead to the conclusions they aim at. That quarrels do not break out when ten children are given ten toys does not rule out the existence of a natural desire for ownership. It means that the desire for ownership may, in healthy cases, be satisfied by absolute equality. The aforesaid example does not rule out the existence of such desire but it may

help to define its nature. Besides, no one can deny that many children would not hesitate to usurp the toys of their friends unless they are prevented from doing so for reasons beyond their control.

3. As to " the angelic era " which the communists suppose to have accompanied the earliest societies, it may be said that there is no real evidence that such an era did really exist. Even if there had been such an era, there could have been no means of production at the time. How could disputes arise over something that did not exist ? At that time people got their food easily and directly from trees. When they went hunting they had to go in groups for fear of wild animals. It was impossible to store slain animals for they would soon go bad. So they had to be eaten up as soon as possible. The absence of conflict in that case does not rule out the existence of a natural desire for ownership. As a matter of fact absence of conflict is due to absence of anything worth the strife. This is why the discovery of agriculture brought about conflict. The said discovery stimulated a hitherto dormant tendency which till then lacked the incentive for action.

4. No one could firmly deny that at such an early era a conflict could have existed among a number of men for the possession of a particular woman. In spite of the existence of sexual communism at that era no one can say for sure that it was prevalent

throughout society or that its existence prevented men from fighting each other for possessing a woman whom they considered very attractive.

This leads to an important conclusion : where all things are equal and similar the possibility of a conflict may be ruled out. But as long as things are different, conflict and struggle are bound to break out even in the imaginary " angelic society " upon which communists build their future prospects.

5. Finally, no one could rule out the fact that some men who lived in that early era desired to achieve personal distinction either by showing their bravery and physical strength or by any other means. Some primitive tribes — examples of the so called " first communist society " — do still refuse to give their daughters in marriage except to those men who would endure a hundred lashes without showing any signs of weariness or pain. There is no doubt that the only reason that invites young men to set for such a painful ordeal is their desire to achieve personal distinction.

If it is true that all things follow a state of absolute equality, we must then search for a reason that leads some people to assert that they are not equal to but even better than others. This leads us to the conclusion that if private ownership is not the outcome of a natural tendency it must be closely connected with another natural tendency namely the desire to achieve personal distinction present in man from time immemorial.

The communists allege that private ownership has been coupled throughout the ages with injustice and therefore if humanity wants to maintain peace and rid itself of bitter conflicts it must abolish private ownership.

But communists seem to forget two important facts : that individual efforts contributed to the progress of humanity and that no progress had been achieved during the so called "angelic era" of "the first communism ? It can be said that humanity started to make any progress only after the existence of conflict over ownership. This means that such conflict is not after all an absolute evil ; on the contrary its existence, within reasonable limits, is a psychological, social and economic necessity.

In addition to this, it should also be borne in mind that Islam does not take it for granted that private ownership underlies all the injustice which afflicted humanity. The serious injustice that accompanied private ownership in Europe and other non-Islamic countries in general was due to the fact that the propertied classes in those countries were themselves the legislators as well as the rulers. It was only natural that such class should make the legislations that safeguarded its interests at the expense of the other classes.

Islam does not recognize the existence of a ruling class. In Islam laws are not made by a specially privileged class; they had been made by God Who created all classes. It is beyond imagination that God should favour some individuals or classes at the expense of others. What reasons could He have for such favouritism ? According to Islam, the ruler is freely elected by all the Muslims. He is not nominated to office by virtue of any class consideration. After assuming the duties of his office, the ruler must follow a law which he did not make, a law that was revealed by God Himself. In this connection we may quote a saying by Abu Bakr, the first Caliph : "Obey me as long as I obey God in my rule over you but where I disobey God you shall not obey me." A ruler in Islam, has no legal power authorising him to confer upon himself or others any legislative privileges. He has no power to prefer one class to another or to act in response to the political influence of the propertied class by enacting legislations which safeguard its interests while oppressing other classes.

It should be pointed out that when we talk about Islamic rule we refer to that period in Islamic history wherein the principles and instructions of Islam were fully applied in their true sense. We do not refer to the periods when corruption changed the system of rule into a monarchy. Islam does not recognize such governments nor can it be held responsible for such rule.

That Islamic rule with all its justice and idealism remained in force only for a brief era should not mean that it is an imaginary system unfit for practical application. After all, what was successfully applied once may be applied again, and it is the duty of all people to work hard for the restoration of such era. The present time, however, is more propitious than ever for the re-establishment of Islamic rule.

Under Islamic rule, the propertied classes will not be given the chance to make laws which serve their interests only. Islam prescribes that all people must be treated according to the same laws without any discrimination regarding human rights or dignity. In case of any differences as to the interpretation of some provisions of law — which happens with respect to every law on earth — the jurisprudents will have the last word. It is to be recorded with pride that the great Muslim jurisprudents did never interpret any law in a manner which might serve the interests of the propertied classes at the expense of the poorer ones. On the contrary they have always been especially inclined to satisfy the basic demands of the working classes and to give them their full due. In fact some Muslim jurisprudents went so far as to regard the workman or the peasant to be in partnership (as far as profits are concerned) with his employer.

On the other hand Islam does not rate human nature so low as to take it for granted that ownership will always inevitably lead to injustice and oppression. In the field of refining and educating human nature Islam achieved an unmatched success. Some Muslims owned property yet " *they entertained no desire in their hearts for that which hath been given them but gave preference to others over themselves though poverty become their lot.*" [1] So they willingly shared their own property with others without expecting any return save forgiveness and recompense from God.

We should always try to remember such noble and lofty examples — rare as they may be. They should be regarded as a ray of light that guides our future steps and unfolds to us the noble achievements which humanity may aspire to realise in future.

It should be understood that Islam never wants us to live in a world of dreams nor does it make the public interest wholly dependent on uncertain " good intentions ". Despite its excessive care for the

---

I.   The **Holy** Quran 59 : 7.

purification and refinement of souls, Islam never forgets practical considerations. Islamic legislation ensures a fair distribution of wealth. By not only concentrating on the purification of the soul but also enacting just legislation, Islam lays the proper foundations for a healthy society. Perhaps this was what Othman Ibn Affan the third Caliph had in mind when he said : " God restrains by power what He does not restrain by the Quran."

To return to the question of ownership, it can be said that ownership existed in certain ages without leading to injustice. Islam permitted ownership of land but never allowed it to lead to feudalism as it did in Europe. Islam took the necessary precautions by enacting economic and social legislations which precluded feudalism and ensured a respectful standard of living even for those who did not own any land. It was such guarantee that protected the poorer class from exploitation by the propertied one.

On the other hand, granting that capitalism might have existed in Islam, it must be understood that Islam would have permitted only such type of capitalism as would serve the public interest. By purifying and refining human nature and at the same time making the necessary legislations, Islam would not have allowed capitalism to grow into an oppressive and exploiting force. By so doing Islam would have relieved the world from the evils which plague the present western world. Besides, the permission of private ownership under Islam was subjected to certain restrictions. It was prescribed for example, that public resources are public property. Where principles of justice required it, Islam prohibited private ownership and permitted it only when satisfactory guarantees had been made against injustice and oppression.

In order to make this point clear, we may borrow an example from non-Muslim countries *i.e.* the Scandinavian states. The English, the Americans and the French — staunch advocates of racial and national discrimination — admit that the Scandinavian peoples are the most civilized and affectionate peoples on earth. It is to be pointed out that such countries have not abolished private ownership but made necessary guarantees for a fair distribution of wealth. Such guarantees bridge the gap between the classes and at the same time prescribe that wages should be proportionate to work. It can be said that the Scandinavian states have in this connection come closer than any other state in the world — to a realisation of some aspects of Islam.

It is impossible to separate any economic system from the social and intellectual philosphies underlying it. If we review the three doctrines that are currently propagated — capitalism, communism and Islam — we shall realise how the economic system and the theory of ownership in each doctrine are closely related to their social background. As previously mentioned, capitalism is based on the assumption that the individual is an inviolable being whose freedom must not be subjected to any social restrictions. It follows that capitalism tends to permit unrestricted private ownership.

On the other hand communism is based on the belief that the community is the base and that the individual has no separate existence of his own. Therefore, communism renders unto the state (as representative of the community) the ownership of all properties, thus depriving all individuals from such right.

Islam holds a different social concept and therefore it adopts a different economic system. With respect to the individual-community relationship, Islam maintains that an individual has two simultaneous capacities : his capacity as an independent individual and his capacity as a member of the community. His response to either capacity may at times be greater than his response to the other one but he will finally combine and harmonise both.

The social concept based on such belief does not separate the individual from his community nor does it regard them as two conflicting forces trying to overcome one another. Since an individual has an independent existence and is at the same time a member of the community it is required of legislation to establish harmony between individual and communal propensities as well as between the interests of each individual and those of others. But such harmony must be achieved without sacrificing either interest for the good of the other. Legislation should not aim at the crushing of individuals for the sake of society nor should it allow society to disintegrate for the sake of one or more individuals.

The economic system of Islam is based on the above mentioned concept of harmony which is some sort of a happy medium between capitalism and communism. It combines the merits of both systems without making the mistakes or deviations of either. It permits private ownership in principle but subjects it to such restrictions as would render it quite harmless. Islam authorises the community and the ruler in his capacity as the representative of the community — to enact the necessary legislation organising ownership and to change such legislation whenever he deems that the public interest requires it.

Islam approves of private ownership since it has the power to eliminate by various means any evils that may result from it. It will be remembered that permission of private ownership in principle while vesting the community with the power to organise and restrict it is a much better arrangement than outright abolition of ownership on the uncertain assumption that it is neither a natural propensity nor a human necessity. The fact that Soviet Russia has had to permit a certain (small) degree of private ownership is a clear evidence that satisfying the propensities of human nature is the best thing for both the individual and public interest.

Why shall we abolish private ownership ? For what ends shall we call upon Islam to do so?

Communism alleges that the abolition of private ownership is the only means to establish equality among people and to suppress the inherent desire for domination and power. Russia abolished ownership of the means of production but has it realised the objectives it hoped to achieve by such abolition ? It will be remembered that Russia under Stalin had to introduce a voluntary overtime work shift for those who had the energy to do it, in return for extra wages. By so doing Russia was creating differences in the wages paid to workers.

Do all people in Russia receive the same wages ? Is it possible that doctors and nurses draw the same salaries ? Communist propagandists often tell us that engineers get the highest wages in Russia and that artists collect the biggest income. By saying this they unwittingly admit the existence of differences in wages among the various classes in Russia. Such differences are noticeable not only among members of the various classes but also among members of the same class.

Has communist Russia managed to wipe out the instinct of domination or the desire to achieve personal distinction? If so, how are trade union leaders, factory managers, senior administrators and commissars selected? How do they sort out active members of the ruling Communist Party?

Apart from the question of the abolition or approval of private ownership should we not admit that the desire for domination and personal distinction is inherent in human nature?

Since the abolition of ownership could not rescue humanity from what communism regards as a great evil why should we follow its example by taking a course that conflicts with human nature and thus attempt to realise an impossible end?

If the communists say that the differences among the classes and the individuals in Russia are too small to lead to luxury or deprivation we may say that — thirteen centuries before communism came into existence — Islam included among its principles the necessity of bridging the gaps among people, prohibiting luxury and wiping out deprivation.

ISLAM AND THE CLASS SYSTEM

Before we discuss Islam's attitude regarding the concept of classes it may be useful to try to understand what is generally meant by a " class system."

In medieval Europe, for instance, there were three distinct classes : the nobility, the clergy and the common people.

The clergy had their own distinctive clothes. In those ages the power of the church was equal and at times opposed to that of kings and emperors. The Pope claimed that it was he who conferred power on kings but they strove to get rid of his influence in order to rule independently. Owing to the property donated by the religious and the exactions imposed on people, the church became so rich that at times it could have armies of its own. On the other hand the nobility inherited nobleness from their forefathers and passed it on to their descendents. A man belonged to the nobility by birth and remained as such until his death regardless of whatever noble or mean actions he might have done in his lifetime.

In the feudal age the nobility exercised absolute powers over the common people who lived in their estates. All the legislative, judicial and executive powers were in their hands. Their whims and fancies were the laws by which they ruled over people. Since representative councils were composed of members belonging to this class, it was only natural that the legislations they made would aim at protecting themselves, safeguarding their own privileges and interests which they surrounded by an air of inviolability.

As for the common people they had no privileges or rights. They inherited poverty, slavery and humiliation and passed them on to their descendents.

The significant economic developments which took place afterwards led to the emergence of the bourgeoisie: the new class which aspired to displace the nobility and to assume their privileges and prestige. It was under the leadership of this emerging class that the common people launched the French Revolution which seemingly abolished the class system and declared , in theory , the principles of liberty, fraternity and equality.

In modern times the capitalist classes have replaced the old nobility. It will be noticed that such replacement took place in a disguised manner and was accompanied by certain changes necessitated by economic development. But the basic principle has never changed. The fact is that the capitalist class still has the property, the power and the ability to steer the government's machinery into the direction they desire. Despite the appearances of freedom manifested in democratic elections, capitalism knows how to sneak into parliaments and government offices in order to achieve its shady ends by crooked means and under various names.

It is to be remembered that a country like Britain — the patron of democracy as we were often told — still has a House of Lords or the Upper house as they call it. Moreover, Britain still applies an ancient feudal law by virtue of which all the property of a dead man passes to his eldest son alone. It is quite clear that such a law aims at keeping estates and properties in the hands of a limited number of people. In this way families' fortunes will not be distributed and such families will retain the old prestige and influence which the feudal classes had in the middle ages.

The class system is based on the wrong assumption that property means power and that the class which owns property has the power as well. Such a class will exercise an influence over the legislative power. Consequently such a class will, by direct or indirect means, make the legislations which protect itself and subject the common people to its own authority, thus depriving them of their legal rights.

In the light of the above mentioned definition of classes it may be truly said **that there has never**

been a class system in Islam. This can be clearly seen from the following facts :

There are no laws in Islam which aim at keeping the property in the hands of particular persons. The Holy Quran plainly says " *In order that it may not merely make a circuit between the wealthy among you* "[1] Therefore, Islam made laws that ensured continual fragmentation and redistribution of wealth. According to the Islamic law of inheritance the inherited property should be distributed among a large number of persons.

An inheritance is never passed on to a single person except in the very rare case where such a person has no brothers, sisters or any other kindred. Even in such rare cases, Islam took the necessary precautions by prescribing that a portion of the inheritance should go to the deprived people who are not related to the dead man. This provision may be regarded as a predecessor of modern inheritance tax. The Holy Quran prescribed that " *if at the time of division (of inheritance) other relatives or orphans or poor are present, feed them out of the (property) and speak to them words of kindness and justice*[2]." It was in this way that Islam solved the problem resulting from the accumulation of property. Property goes

---

1. (59 : 7).
2. (4 : 8).

to individuals as such and not as members of a particular class, because when they die the property will be redistributed according to new proportions. History bears witness that property in the Islamic society was constantly exchanging hands without being confined to a particular faction of the nation.

This leads to an important conclusion : Legislation in Islam is not the prerogative of a particular class. In the Islamic state no one is allowed to make the legislations he desires because all people are treated according to the same Islamic laws which were revealed by God and which hold no distinctions among people.

It follows that the Islamic society is a classless society. It will be understood that existence of classes is closely connected with the existence of a legislative prerogative. Where such a privilege is non-existent, and no one can make legislations which safeguard his own interests at the expense of others, there will be no classes.

✳

Now let us explain how two relevant verses which, if read carelessly, might lead to some doubts.

" *God has bestowed his gifts of sustenance more freely on some of you than on others* "[1].

" *We raised some of them above others in ranks* "[2].

---

1. (16 : 71).
2. (43 : 32).

Do such verses mean that Islam recognizes the class system ?

These two verses merely describe what is actually taking place on earth be it under Islamic rule or otherwise. They state that people differ in rank and livelihood. Let us take Russia for example. Do all people get the same wages or are some people more privileged than others in livelihood ? Are all the conscripted people made officers or soldiers or are some of them raised above others in rank ? The existence of differences among people is an inevitable fact. The two verses do not give a particular reason for such differences. They do not even state that such preference is based on capitalist, communist or even Islamic considerations. They do not say that such preference may be just or unjust by our standards. The two verses merely say that such preference exists everywhere on earth. But of course, all that takes place on earth falls within the sphere of God's will.

It must have become clear by now that the Islamic society is a society without classes or legislative privileges. It will be noticed that the existence of differences in wealth and property should not be confused with the question of classes unless such property and wealth conferred upon their owners any legislative and in-

dividual privileges. Differences in wealth will not
lead to the emergence of classes so long as all people
are — actually not in theory only — equal before
the law.

It should be pointed out that the ownership
of land under Islam did not confer upon land owners
any special privileges or rights by which they might
enslave or exploit others. The same thing would have
happened if capitalism had existed in a truly Islamic
society, especially because the ruler does not derive
his power from the propertied class but he is elected
by the nation and is carrying out the law of God.

In addition to the above mentioned, there can
be no community wherein wealth will be equally
distributed among all individuals; surely not
in the communist society which, truly or not,
claims to have abolished the class system though in
fact it has left one ruling class which suppresses all
other classes.

ISLAM AND ALMS

The communists as well as some of those whose souls and thoughts were enthralled by colonialism try to accuse Islam of letting the common people lead a life of dependence on the alms given by the rich. This false accusation is derived from the mistaken belief that Azzakat is an alms obligingly donated by the wealthy people.

In refuting such accusations we should distinguish between Azzakat and alms. Charity is voluntary. It cannot be imposed by law or by order of the ruler. Azzakat, on the other hand, is an ordinance prescribed by law ; the government must fight those who refuse to pay Azzakat and may even kill them if they persist in such refusal, because they would then be considered apostates. It is needless to say that nothing of the sort would happen with respect to charity which is completely left to our own consciences.

From the financial point of view, Azzakat was the first regular tax ever imposed in the world. Before that taxes were imposed according to the whims of rulers. The exaction of such taxes was affected by the ruler's need for money to achieve personal ambitions. The burden of taxation used to fall on the poor rather than the rich and very often the taxes were collected from the common people alone. Islam organized the collection of taxes and prescribed a maximum percentage which may not be exceeded in ordinary circumstances. Taxes were imposed on the rich and middle classes but the poor were exempted.

It should be borne in mind that Islam prescribes that the proceeds of Azzakat should be distributed among the poor by the state and not by the rich people. In this sense, Azzakat is a tax collected and distributed by the state. The Public Treasury under Islam is the counterpart of the modern Ministry of Finance which collects the public revenues and distributes them among the various public utilities. The state supports and looks after those who become needy — through inability to earn their living or due to the insufficiency of their means — but it cannot be said that the state does that out of charity or that such help is humiliating to the recipients. No one can say that retired officials who receive pensions from the state or that workmen who benefit from social security schemes feel like begging from the rich. The same thing can be said of helpless children and aged people who cannot earn their living. No one can say that the pride of such people is hurt when the state supports and extends aid to them. The state is bound to do such things by virtue of its human obligations.

Social security by the state is a modern system which humanity managed to adopt after bitter experiences and a long history of social injustice. One of the glories of Islam is that it prescribed the said system at a time when Europe lived in social darkness. Yet some people who are charmed by systems which are imported from the West or East, accuse the same systems of regression and backwardness if they had been adopted by Islam.

It should be pointed out that if the circumstances of life in the early years of Islam necessitated or tolerated that the poor may personally receive Azzakat in cash or in kind, nothing in the provisions of Islam prescribes that the aforesaid method is the only way for the distribution of Alzakat. Therefore, nothing in Islam prevents the use of Azzakat funds in building hospitals and schools from which people may benefit or in the establishment of cooperative societies which can make life easier for the poorer people or in the construction of factories which provide permanent employment for many people. In other words, the proceeds of Azzakat may be given in the form of social services. Only those who are incapacitated through illness, old age or childhood, are entitled to receive Azzakat in cash but others may receive it in the form of employment or social services.

Besides, the Islamic society is not supposed to comprise any poor people who might live in complete dependence on Azzakat.

It is good to remember that the Islamic society reached an ideal stage during the age of Omar bin Abdel Aziz. Azzakat was collected, yet the collectors could not find any one who would accept it or any poor people among whom they might distribute it. Let us listen to what was said by Yehia bin Said, a zakat collector under Omar bin Abdel Aziz : " Omar bin Abdel Aziz sent me to collect alms from Africa. I collected the alms and then looked for the poor to distribute the alms among them but I found none, nor I found anyone who might have accepted them from me, for Omar bin Abdel Aziz had enriched the people."

There is no doubt that every community is likely to comprise poor and needy people. Therefore, the necessary legislation should be made to face such a problem. It should be borne in mind that Islam constantly attached to itself new communities at different degrees of richness. It was only natural that legislation should be made which would help to lead gradually to the ideal stage which existed under the rule of Omar bin Abdel Aziz.

ALMS :

Alms are the properties which the rich voluntarily give for the sake of charity. Islam approved and encouraged almsgiving. Alms were supposed to be given in various ways : by supporting parents and relatives, and helping the needy in general. It may also take the form of good deeds or kind words.

No one can say that being generous to our relatives hurts their feeling or insults their pride. Such generosity to our relatives is the outcome of affection, sympathy and compassion. When you present a gift to your brother or give a dinner in honour of your relatives you will not be humiliating them or arousing their malignance or hatred.

As for the gifts in kind which are given to the needy, they are subject to the same prescriptions which governed Azzakat in the early days of Islam. Circumstances of life at that time tolerated the donation of gifts in kind and Islam regarded such gifts as honest means to help the needy and those in trouble. Nothing in Islam prescribed that alms should be given in one form only. Alms may be given in the form of donations to societies and organizations which provide social services. Azzakat may be given as an aid to any Islamic state which needs funds for the execution of its schemes and enterprises. Islam maintains that as long as there are poor people, the state should try by all possible means to make their life more comfortable. Besides, the Islamic society is not supposed to comprise any poor people. When the Islamic state reaches the above mentioned ideal stage, many people may not be in need of alms just as they at one time did not need Azzakat. In such case, both Azzakat and alms will be allocated for services that are of great importance to every community *i.e.* looking after people who are unable to work for any reason whatsoever.

It will be noticed that Islam has never called upon Muslims to lead a life of dependence on charity. The Islamic state is required to secure honourable life for those who are unable to earn their living, it being understood that such obligation is not the outcome of charity or condescension.

On the other hand, the Islamic state is required to provide suitable work for every person who is able to work. The state's obligation to find work for every Muslim is emphasized by the following tradition :—

> " *A man came to the Prophet (peace and prayer of God be upon him) begging for anything to live on. The Prophet gave him an axe and a rope and ordered him to collect some wood and sell it and live by its price. He further told the man to come back and report what would happen to him.*"

Now, some misguided people may be inclined to say that the above mentioned tradition is just an individual example of no significance in the twentieth century. They would also say that the said example involved an axe, a rope and one man whereas the

modern life involves great factories, millions of unemployed workers and organized governments whose
functions are carried out by various competent departments.

Such logic is surely a naive one. The Prophet
was not required to talk about factories or lay down
the necessary legislation a thousand years before the
existence of any factories. If he had done so no one
would have understood him.

It was quite sufficient that he laid down the basic
principles of legislation, leaving for each generation
the task of devising their suitable method of application
within the framework of the basic principles.

The above mentioned tradition contains the
following basic principles :

1. Sense of responsibility by the Prophet (*i.e.* head
   of the state) for finding work for the man.

2. The Prophet ensured work for that man
   (according to the circumstances existing at
   that time.)

3. The Prophet emphasized his sense of responsibility by ordering the man to come back
   and report what would happen to him.

This sense of responsibility which Islam prescribed thirteen centuries ago is completely supported by
the most modern economic and political theories.

But where the state is unable to find work for the unemployed, the Public Treasury will support them until their circumstances improve. There is nothing wrong in this for Muslims are generous to themselves, to the state and to others.

ISLAM AND WOMAN

The East today is simmering with a furore over the rights of woman and a demand in her behalf for a perfect equality with men. The most noteworthy among the feverous champions of women's rights are those men and women who in the name of Islam rave most foolishly, some mischievously alleging that Islam has in all respects maintained a perfect equality between the sexes, while others, thanks to their ignorance of Islam or a negligence thereof, claim that Islam is an enemy of woman, for it degrades her and lowers her status holding her intellectually deficient and assigning her a position very much akin to that of animals. She is reduced to no more than a mere means of sensual gratification for man and a machine for the propagation of the human species ; which is sufficient to show how subservient to man she is in the sight of Islam with the result that man dominates her and enjoys an all-round superiority over her.

Both of these classes of people are equally ignorant of Islam or they intentionally confuse the right with the wrong in order to deceive others and sow the seeds of discord and mischief in society so as to further their own nefarious designs and facilitate the foul game they are out to play.

Before embarking upon a detailed discussion of the position of woman in Islam, we propose first to touch in brief upon the history of the movement for woman emancipation in Europe, for it is this very source of mischief whence all the defecting trends in the modern East flow.

The woman in Europe and all over the world was looked upon as a mere nonentity. She formed the theme of many a discourse of the learned " scholars " and " philosophers " who wrangled among themselves over questions such as these: Has woman got a soul or not ? If yes, then what precisely is the nature of her soul, is it human or animal ? Supposing she does possess a human soul then what social and human position should she occupy in relation to man ? Is she born as a slave to man or does she hold a position slightly superior to that of a slave ?

This situation remained unchanged even through those relatively short spans of history when woman appears to have occupied a central position in the social set-up of the times e.g. in Greece and the Roman Empire. But all this exaltation did not mean the exaltation of woman as such ; it was rather an ex-altation of a few outstanding women inhabiting in the capital cities because of some of their personal qualities which made them the life and soul of social parties. They were no more than means of diversion and entertainment for the licentious rich who applauded their appearances in public out of sheer vanity and self-conceit. But this did not signify any respect towards woman as a human being and apart from the pleasure she brought to men.

This position of woman in Europe remained unaltered during the periods of serfdom and feudalism. She in her ignorance was blandished sometimes by luxury and licence and at times was content to live as animals, eating, drinking, bearing children, giving birth to others, and working day and night.

When the industrial revolution took place in Europe it brought in its wake the worst possible sufferings for woman yet experienced by her throughout the history of mankind.

Europe has throughout the ages exhibited such a rigidity and avarice of nature as lacks both generosity and liberality. It made men undergo hardships without a promise of any immediate or remote material gains in return. However, the economic conditions of life during the periods of slavery and feudalism along with the prevalent agricultural milieu were such as made man responsible for the support of woman. It was quite natural and in complete harmony with the spirit of the age. The woman nonetheless at that time worked at some simple cottage industries such as are found in any agricultural society. In this way she paid back the price to men for supporting her.

But with the industrial revolution the whole of the social scene underwent a radical change in the country no less than in cities. The family life was completely ruined, and the ties holding together its members were torn as under when women and children were, thanks to the industrial revolution, forced to go out and work in factories. The working classes slowly and gradually left the country life, a life based on the principles of mutual responsibility and co-operation, and came over to cities where everybody lived a solitary life and where nobody was interested in his neighbours nor anyone in a mood to support others but worked and earned to support his own-self. Here, there were no more any rules of morality observed or cared for. Men and women no longer bothered about moral scruples if they but once found any opportunity to gratify their sexual urge. As a result thereof the will to marry and support a family suffered a decline among these people or if it still persisted in some hearts the trend was to postpone it at least for some years longer.[1]

We do not intend in these pages to dwell on the history of Europe. We are merely concerned with the factors that influenced the career of woman in European history. As we said above the industrial revolution overburdened woman and children with work. This weakened family ties, which in turn led to a complete disintegration of family life. But it was the woman who had to pay dearly. She worked harder than ever before, and lost her honour, but was still far from being satisfied psychologically and materially. Man not only shrank back from taking upon himself the responsibility for supporting her — be she his wife, or mother — but also charged her to provide for

---

[1] It is on the basis of such evidence that the proponents of materialism and marxism claim that the economic conditions alone engender the social conditions of life and that only the economic circumstances determine the mutual relations of men. We do not deny the importance of the economic factor in human life, but it is wrong to say that it is the economic factor alone which determines the thoughts, feelings and behaviour of men. The fact that the economic factor exercised such a dominating influence over the European life was due to the absence of any lofty ideal such as might have—as it did in the Islamic World—elevated Europe spiritually, thus enabling Europeans to base their economic relationship on a purely human basis. In this way it would have not only realized its economic requirements but the people all over the world would have also been spared the trouble it made them suffer due to its lust for exploitation.

her ownself. In the factories she was exploited most ruthlessly by the factory owners ; she worked there for long hours but was paid far less than the men doing a kindred job in that very factory.

It is needless to ask why this all happened as we know that Europe has been for ever known for its miserliness, rigidity, and ingratitude. It has never been known to respect men as men, nor to render a voluntary act of goodness where it could with impunity inflict others with evil as its record of the past as well as of the present testifies; and it might as well remain unchanged in the years to come except if God Almighty should lead it to the right path and elevate it spiritually. However weak and helpless they were, women and children suffered a most ruthless exploitation.

There were, however, some conscientious men who could not silently forbear the perpetration of these vile inequities against the weaker sections of the population. They struggled to put an end to this cruelty towards the children (please note, the children, not women !) The social reformers denounced the employing of children as workers in factories at an early age, burdening them with work that retarded their natural growth besides paying them scanty and inadequate wages for the burdensome and rough work they did. The protests against social injustice did not however go unnoticed. They bore fruit ; the age of employment was gradually raised ; the wages were increased, and the working hours were cut down.

But women still remained without anyone to champion or advance their cause, as it required an intellectual refinement such as Europe did not possess. As a result thereof woman pressed on her way through this ordeal overworking herself in a desperate effort to support herself but receiving in return wages far less than those given to her male counterpart — for a similar work.

In the first great war tens of millions of European and American young men were killed leaving behind them millions of widowed women. These poor women suffered the worst tribulations and trials of labour. They had none to support or look after them, for the bread-winners of most of these families were either killed in war or crippled for life, or had suffered such a nervous breakdown because of fear, nervous tension or poisonous gases as had left them incapacitated for work, or they had just been released from a prison house after serving a four years' term and now would enjoy themselves to regain their nervous self-composure. All such people had lost the will to get married and support a whole family, thus putting themselves to physical as well as material inconvenience.

The war had caused so great a shortage of men that the survivors could hardly supply their place. The factories could not restart their production nor could the war damages be repaired due to the shortage of working hands. Thus it fell upon women to go out and take the place of men, for if they did not, they as well as their dependents — old women and small children — were threatened by hunger. To go and work in the factories however, required that woman should ignore her moral temperament as well as her feminine nature which had now become a positive hurdle in earning her living. Moreover factory owners did not want working hands merely; they wanted to satisfy their lust as well. The helplessness of woman now promised them an excellent opportunity of which they fully availed themselves. The woman thus had to discharge a two-fold duty : work in the factories , and try her level best to please her employer. The woman was not plagued by hunger alone; sex too claimed its share and gratification. As the number of men had fallen too low due to the war, not all the women could achieve that gratification through marriage. But creed and religion prevalent in Europe did not allow polygamy — as Islam does — in such periods of emergency. Thus the woman in Europe was left at the mercy of her passions that swept her away bongre' malgre'. Her need for bread and the urge to achieve sexual gratification besides her love for costly clothes, cosmetics etc. were the factors that forced her to this course of life.

Thus did the western woman persist in this course of life pleasing men, working in factories and shops and achieving the things she admired by foul or fair means. But the more she came to possess them, the intenser her passion for them grew, for the satisfaction of which she was egged on to work more. The factory owners exploited this weakness of woman to their own advantage. They paid her wages far less than those they paid to the male workers doing the same work at the same factory — a gross inequity which neither reason, nor conscience of mankind can ever justify.

Under these circumstances the stupendous revolution that at last broke out in Europe was but inevitable. It swept away the centuries-old inequity and gross injustice.

But what did woman get as a result of this revolution ? She was over-worked physically, had lost respect as well as her womanhood ! She was denied even the natural pleasure of having a family, having children, living with them and of realizing her own true self by suffering for them and so have a true sense of well-being and magnanimity. She did however in place of these at last win the right to have equal wages with man, the only natural right offered her by Europe.

The European man did not however easily forego his superiority — his egoism rather — with respect to woman. He was forced to recognize equal rights for her after a very tough and intense struggle in which all the usual weapons of warfare were fully made use of.

In this struggle for her rights the woman resorted to strikes and co-operation ; addressed public meetings , and employed journalism to advance her cause. Then she realized that in order to set things right she would have to participate in legislation as well, so first she demanded the right to vote and then proceeded to ask for a right to become a member of the parliament. As she had received an education similar to that imparted to man, for both were required to do similar jobs, now as a logical sequence to it she demanded an equal share in government along with men.

Such is the story of woman's struggle in Europe to obtain her rights. It is one continuous story all the different episodes of which are intimately linked together. Whether man liked all this or not is immaterial but woman too was to realise shortly that she was as helpless as man in this new degenerated social order where she had successfully ousted man from the position of leadership and authority.[1]

---

[1]   It is on the basis of such evidence that the Marxists claim that the economic factor is the only real factor in life as in fact it was that very factor that determined the course of the problem of woman in Europe. As we said somewhere before we admit the importance of the economic factor in life, but we hold that the course of circumstances in Europe would have been a different one if it had an ideology and system of life like Islam which enjoins upon man to support woman in all circumstances and which gives woman in case she is at all driven to work for her self, an equal right to have wages similar to those of man, and which to meet an emergency provided for polygamy. as successful and clean solution of the crisis generally met with after wars making it all the more necessary for woman to take up arduous and difficult jobs, satisfying her natural sexuality by a resort to foul and ugly course.

But despite all this the readers will be surprised to learn that even today in England — the cradle of democracy — women serving in government departments continue to receive less pay from Government than men do, although there are already so many honourable lady-members in the British parliament.

Let us take up the position of woman in Islam and see if there are any historical, geographical, economical, ideological and legal conditions such as should force woman to take up arms for her rights like her counterpart in the West. Or is it merely an inferiority complex and a result of thoughtlessly imitating the West that makes these Eastern champions of her rights declaim so enthusiastically in public meetings ?

As a fundamental principle of its system, Islam holds that woman is a human being ; and she has a soul similar to that of men : *" O People ! be careful of (your duty to) your Lord, who created you from a single being and created its mate of the same (kind) and spread from these two many men and women."* [1] Thus men and women were quite equal to each other in their origin, their abode as well as in their place of return and were as such entitled to similar and equal rights. Islam gave her the right to life, to honour, and to property like men. She was a respectable being

---

1. The Holy Quran (4 : 1)

and it was not permissible for any one to find fault with her or backbite her. No one was also to spy on her or hold her in contempt due to her functions as a woman. These were the rights that both men and women enjoyed, there being no differentiation against either of them. The law laid down about these applied to men and women alike ; *"O ye who believe ! Let not some men among you laugh at others : it may be that the (latter) are better than the (former): nor let some women laugh at others, it may be that the latter are better than the (former) : nor defame nor be sarcastic to each other, nor call each other by (offensive) nick-names*[1]*"* *".... and spy not on each other, nor speak ill of each other behind their backs."*[2] *"O you who believe ! do not enter houses other than your own houses until you have asked permission and saluted their inmates."* [3] The Holy Prophet said : *" It is forbidden for a Muslim to take the life, honour and property of another Muslim."* (Bukhari and Muslim).

The reward for both sexes for their good acts is also similar : *" And their Lord hath heard them (and He sayeth): Lo ! I suffer not the work of any worker, male or female, to be lost. Ye proceed one from another."* (3 : 285).

Men and women are also equal in their rights to realize their material needs in the world including similar rights to hold property, and dispose of it as they should wish. They are free to mortgage it, to

1. The Holy Quran (49 : 11)
2. Ibid   (49 : 11)
3. Ibíd   (24 : 27)

give it in lease, or bequeath it, sell or buy it or exploit it for his or her own benefit : *" unto the men belongeth a share of that which parents and near kindred leave, and unto the women a share of that which parents and near kindred leave."* (4 : 7), and *"unto men a fortune from that which they have earned, and unto women a fortune from that which they have earned."* (4 : 32).

We must pause here awhile to take note of two important points concerning woman's right to hold property and use or exploit it at will. The legal systems of the " civilized " Europe till very recently did not give any of these rights to woman. She could exercise these rights only indirectly through a man, her husband, father or guardian. This means in other words that even after Islam had granted woman these rights, the woman in Europe was deprived of them for more than eleven hundred years. And when she at last secured them she did not do so easily, nor could she during this hard struggle for her rights keep intact her innate character, honour and nobleness of person. She had rather to forego all of these virtues besides experiencing a gruesome chain of hard work, murders, privations and miseries in order to obtain what was no more than a mere portion of what Islam had already granted to women folk, not due to the pressure of some economic circumstances, or as a result of the inter-class conflict going on in the world. It was rather initiated by its desire to implement truth and justice, the two most cardinal facts of human life — in practice rather than in the world of dreams.

In the second place, we must also take note of the fact that communism in particular and the West in general holds that human life is synonymous to man's economic existence. Thus they say that so long as woman did not hold any right to ownership or exploit freely what she possessed she had no independent existence at all and that she attained a human status only after she came to have an independent economic existence, that is when she at last came to possess the right to hold property directly and not through man and was free to use or enjoy it, as she thought fit.

Notwithstanding the fact that we do not agree to such a narrow view of human life and its degradation to a pure economic existence we do however agree in principle with these people — the communists and the western thinkers—that a sound economic standing does affect human feelings and the growth of self consciousness in human beings. Islam occupies a unique position in that it recognized an independent economic status of woman aud gave her the right to own, use and enjoy it in her own right without any intermediary trustee or mediator. Not only this but in the most important problem of her life *i.e.* marriage, as well her independent status was established. She could not be given in marriage without her assent ; no marriage was valid unless she agreed to it. The Holy Prophet says : " *No widow should be married without consulting her ; and no virgin be married without her assent, and her assent is her silence.*" (Bukhari and Muslim). Even after the marriage ceremony if she declared that she did not assent to it, the marriage is dissolved.

Before Islam woman had to adopt a round about and crooked course to free herself of her husband who held her in a state of perfect subservience, for neither the law of the land nor the common law gave her the right to leave her husband by securing a separation. Islam gave her this right in clear and unequivocal terms which she could exercise whenever she had a mind to.(1) Not content with this, Islam even went a step further giving her the right to propose her marriage to any man she liked to marry. The European woman obtained this right only in the eighteenth century and still it was hailed there as a very great victory for woman against the centuries old traditions of the past !

(I)   Such a right of woman at the first glance may appear as a mere illusion in the context of the present socio-economic conditions of life in the East but Islam cannot be blamed for acts that contradict its teachings or bar the way to the implementation of its laws. Woman did in the early period of Islam exercise this right and it was acknowledged by the Holy Prophet, the law maker as well as his successors, the early caliphs. What we demand today is the implementation of all these laws along with the removal of all those obstacles that intervene in their promulgation be they economic and social circumstances or the un-Islamic practices followed blindfoldly in imitation of others.

Again it was Islam that at a period when the entire world was lost in ignorance and darkness stressed the importance of knowledge for mankind, not as a special privilege of a particular class but as an essential and unavoidable need for each and every man. Islam made it obligatory upon Muslims to acquire knowledge as a necessary condition to their being true believers in God and Islam. It also goes to the credit of Islam that it was the first religion that acknowledging a separate and independent human status of woman impressed upon her that she could not achieve perfection without knowledge. Acquisition of knowledge was as great a duty of woman as of man, for Islam wanted the women-folk to develop their rational faculties along with their physical ones and thus ascend to higher planes of spiritual existence, whilst on the other hand Europe did not even recognize any such right for woman till very recently and did in the end grant it to her only when compelled by the pressure of economic circumstances.

What we have said above is sufficient to confute the allegation that Islam accords woman only a secondary status or that she is treated as subservient to man or that her role in life is in the eyes of Islam, of no importance at all. For if it had been so, Islam would not have attached so great an importance to the acquisition of knowledge for woman. That it did so goes to prove that Islam acknowledges an honourable and noble status for woman in life — in the eyes of God as well as society.

But after acknowledging a perfectly equal status as human beings for both men and women, and treating them as equals, entitled to equal rights, Islam does however differentiate between man and woman with regard to their special functions in life, a step that has given rise to a great hue and cry by some women organisations supported by certain writers, " reformers " and young men.

Before we consider the points on which Islam differentiates between the sexes, let us first tackle the basic problem from physiological, biological and psychological stand-points. After that we will take up the Islamic view-point.

Do men and women belong in one and the same sex or are they two distinct sexes ? Have they got similar functions in life or are their functions separate and distinct as man and woman ? This is in fact the knotty point, the crux of the problem. If the women conferences, their supporters, the writers, the reformers and the young men mean to say that there is no difference whatsoever in the physical and intuitional equipment of man and woman as well as in their biological functions in life, then we have nothing to say to them. But if they acknowledge that a difference does exist between man and woman and their respective functions, we may yet fruitfully discuss the problem together.

The problem of equality of the two sexes, I have already dealt with at great length in my book " Man Between Islam and Materialism" (الانسان بين المادية والاسلام). It may not be amiss to reproduce some paragraphs from it here below :—

"And as a consequence ofthis fundamental difference in their functions and objectives we find that man and woman have so come to differ from each other in disposition as well as in constitution that each is equipped with what it can suitably accomplish its respective primary functions.

" It is for this reason that I am at a loss to understand how all this empty talk about an absolute equality between man and woman can ever bring it to pass. The demand for equality between man and woman as human beings is a natural and reasonable demand. Man and woman are two equally important component parts of a whole humanity, proceeding from the one and the same progenitor. But so far as the demand for treating them as equals in their functions in life and the modes of their actual performance is concerned, can that ever be feasible ? That is simply impossible even if all the women around the world should wish it, hold conferences and pass resolutions to that effect. These conferences and their resolutions cannot alter the innate characters of men and women, nor can they in any way transform their functions making men share those of women in conception, birth and suckling and vice versa.

" No specific biological function can be carried out in the absence of a special type of psycho-physical disposition. This means, in other words, that the specialized functions of woman viz. conceiving and suckling, call for the emotional-cum-intellectual outfit of a special type such as prepares and enables her to discharge these most arduous duties.

" Of course, motherhood with all its noble feelings, exalted acts, patience through a series of tribulations, besides a most meticulous perfection in consideration and performance, cannot exist in the absence of that physical constitution which befits a woman for her specialized functions of conceiving and suckling and gives form to her psychological, intellectual as well as nervous organism. These intellectual, psychological, nervous and physical characteristics of woman — are found side by side complementing one another as well as co-ordinating and harmonising themselves. Therefore, it must be a very rare exception that one of them should exist without a simultaneous existence of its counterparts.

"And all this tenderness of feelings, intuitional impressibility, and highly susceptible disposition with which a woman is endowed show that basically she possesses an emotional character rather than an intellectual one. It is this very emotional character that forms the most lively and ever flowing spring of her motherly attributes, as the upbringing of a child calls for qualities not intellectual which may be passive or active and may or may not successfully meet the requirements of a child, but an overflow of vehement feelings and passions such as does not allow her to meditate coolly but impels her to answer the child's call immediately without delay or slackness."

" This in fact is the true character of woman in life. It helps her in the performance of her real functions as well as in the realization of her creative purpose."

" Man, on the other hand, has to discharge a quite different duty for which he is equipped aptly but differently from woman. He has to engage in the struggle of life going on in the outside world, be it in the form of subduing wild beasts in jungles, or contending against the forces of nature on earth and heavens, or forming of a government, or legislating about national economy. He has to tackle all these problems to scratch a living and safeguard his person, his wife as well as his children against oppression."

" Man as such does not need the vehement emotional nature for the performance of his functions in life. Emotions prove harmful rather than helpful in pursuance of his duties, for they are characterised with a fickleness that causes them change rapidly and into mutually quite contradictory states of mind. They are unable to pursue a course of action for long. The objects attracting them ever change. Such an ever-changing emotional character is suitable for motherhood that has got to deal with mutually opposed and changing situations. But they are not helpful for man whose work demands of him constancy and steadfastness for long periods of time. Rather it is his intellectual disposition that proves helpful to him in a practical life where he has to contend against so many adverse forces. He has thus more efficiency in planning, in carefully revising the situation and taking note of all the possible consequences of his scheme before actually translating it into action. The intellect moves slowly but steadily, for quickness and rapidity of action are not expected of it as against the vehement emotions that lend colour to the whole existence of woman. What is however expected of intellect is that it should show a most proper way to achieve its end be it the hunting of a beast, inventing of an instrument, laying down the foundations of a new system of economy, setting up a new form of government, kindling a war, or making peace. All these activities of man depend upon his intellectual ability. Emotions creeping in cannot but spoil them."

" And therefore man is well adjusted only when he is engaged in his true manly pursuits and objectives in life. This should explain the various differences found in the respective constitutions of man and woman : why it is that man joyfully pursues the professions where he has mostly to draw on his physical and intellectual faculties whereas in emotional life he is just as mercurial as a child ; and why it is that a woman is adjusted in her natural sphere of emotional activities only and derives so great a pleasure out of these, for it is through these alone that she can best realize the real objective of her earthly existence. That is also why she feels at ease in those professions only that have got an emotional appeal for her feminine nature viz. nursing, teaching or fostering. Similarly when she goes to work in a shop, it is because it has also got an emotional charm of its own for her as it enables her to carry out her search for a male companion. But all these activities are mere off-shoots ; they cannot in themselves however satisfy her innate urge for a husband, a home, a family and children. It is natural therefore that as soon as she gets a chance to perform her primary functions, she leaves off her job and devotes herself exclusively to her household duties unless compelled otherwise by an exigency such as the need for money etc.

" This does not however mean that man and woman are fundamentally and irreconcilably different from each other. Nor does it imply that all the members of a sex lack all the potentialities necessary for the functions which the members of the opposite sex alone by nature are fit to perform.

"The two sexes are thus found mixed up, as if it were, in a medley. If you find a woman who is capable of ruling, dispensing justice, lifting heavy burdens and fighting in wars ...... and if you come across a man who can cook, do household chores or has got very tender motherly feelings for children or is very fickle emotionally and is visited by shifting moods, then you must remember that it is all natural ; there is nothing unnatural about it. It is the logical result of the fact that each sex has in itself the germs of both sexes. But this does not at all prove what these misguided westerners and the discordant easterners would have us believe. The real problem stated briefly rather is : can all these extra-functions that a woman is called upon to perform substitute for her real and natural function ? Does she in the presence of these no longer feel the desire for a home, children and a family ? Above all does she no longer feel the need for a male partner for the gratification of her sex instinct ? "

Now that we know the reality of differences between man and woman, let us return to the points that form the basis of differentiation between the two sexes and their functions in Islam.

The great distinctive mark of Islam is that it is a practical system of life and is ever ready to make due allowance for the human nature never seeking to oppose or make it deviate from its natural course. It calls upon men to purify their souls and makes them ascend to such higher planes of being as approximate the realm of ideals and dreams, but in the whole process of improving and edifying men, it does not seek to alter their basic natures, nor does it believe that such a change in human nature is ever possible or useful for the welfare of mankind, if ever possible. It rather believes that the noblest achievements of humanity are those that it achieves through and with the help of its own basic nature after its refinement and ascension to the noblest planes of voluntary virtue from being a mere captive of its material needs.

The attitude adopted by Islam about the problem of man and woman too is quite in line with the human nature. Thus it effects equality between them where there is a natural ground for it ; and differentiates between them where such a differentiation is but natural. Let us take up two outstanding situations in which Islam differentiates between the sexes : the distribution of inheritance ; and the headship of the family.

About inheritance Islam says : " *To the male the equivalent of the portion of two females,*" which is quite natural and justified, for it is man alone who is charged with shouldering all the financial obliga- tions. The woman is under no such obligation as to spend money on anyone but her own person and toilet, except of course when she should head her family but such a situation is very rarely met with in an Islamic society, for so long as a woman has got a relation howsoever distant she need not take upon herself the support of her family. Can such an arrangement be termed as injustice towards woman, as the votaries of feminism aver ? Leaving aside these vain postulations and prejudiced claims, the problem is just one of a simple reckoning : on the whole woman gets one third of the inherited property to spend it on her person, whereas man is given two thirds of it to discharge his financial obligations in the first place, towards, his wife, (that is the woman), and secondly his family and children. As such, speaking in terms of simple mathematics, to whom does the larger portion go ? There may be certain men who are wont to spend all their money on themselves and are disinclined to marry or found a family, but such cases are uncommon. Normally it is the man who shoulders the financial burdens of his family, including a woman, his wife, not as an act of grace but as a moral obligation. If a woman possesses a property of her own, her husband cannot take it away from her without her consent; he would even then have to bear her financial burden, as if it were, she had nothing in her possession to support herself with. And if he should refuse her this allowance or should he be miserly in proportion to his income she can lodge a complaint against him in the court and force him to give her the sustenance allowance or get free from him. There is as such no justification to say that in inheritance woman receives a share less than that of man, as in view of his obligations it is but natural that a man should get double the share of a woman.

Islam maintains a similar proportion in the distribution of a bequest. The law followed here is one of the fairest ones yet known to mankind : " For every person according to his needs," the standard to determine the need being the social burdens that one has to bear. But so far as their earnings are concerned there is no difference between man and woman ; nor in their wages for a work, nor in the profit gained in trade, nor in revenues from land etc., for, in these matters Islam follows another law, the law treating on a perfectly equal footing man and woman with regard to their labours and the wages thereof. No injustice is to be done to either of them. The impression generally current among the common masses of Muslims and purposely spread by the antagonists of Islam that in the eyes of Islam woman is worth half of what man is worth, is false as we have shown above by a simple mathematical calculation.

That the evidence of two women is in Islam equivalent to that of one man also does not prove that woman is no better than a half man. It is rather a wise step to secure and preserve the genuine character of legal evidence in courts through all possible means and against all possible perversities irrespective of the fact whether the evidence is for or against the accused. The woman is by her very nature vehemently emotional, impressionable and liable to digress from the real facts of the case in hand. Therefore it is wise to have another woman along with her " *so if the one erreth the other will remember,*" for it is quite possible that the accused, against or for whom a woman appears as a witness, may be an attractive woman which may make the witness jealous and hostile towards her and so give a wrong evidence; or again may be that the accused is a young man whose sight may so arouse the mother in the witness that knowingly or unknowingly she proffers evidence that is false. But it is very rare that two women appearing before court at once should fall a prey to such an error, both of them offering false evidences. The chances in such situations are rather that if one of them is deceived or confused about truth, her companion may correct her. It must however be added here that a single woman's evidence is quite dependable if the witness concerned be a specialist in female diseases and she appears as a witness in a case concerning these.

Now as to the second problem, the headship of the family, it is quite clear that it requires a manager to look after and manage the affairs of the family, which represents an association of man, woman and children with the attendant obligations springing therefrom. Like every other social organization, the family too stands in need of a responsible head in the absence of whom a state of anarchy is bound to prevail, which may ultimately lead to a general privation of all. There may be three possibilities as to the headship of the family: one, man is the head of the family ; second, woman heads it ; and third, both of them are at once the heads of the family.

We need not take into account the third and the last possibility as our common experience is enough to show that the presence of two heads always leads to even more trouble and anarchy than when there is no head at all. The Holy Quran referring to the creation of the earth and heavens says : " *If there were therein Gods beside Allah, then verily both (the heavens and the earth) had been disordered ;* " " *Nor is there any God along with Him ; else would each God have assuredly championed that which He created, and some of them would assuredly overcome others.*"[1] If such is the case with these imaginary Gods, then what about human beings who are so aggressive and unjust ?

The science of psychology bears witness that the children brought up under quarrelsome parents wrangling over the headship of the family are found to be unbalanced emotionally besides being victims to so many psychological complexes and disorders.

There are thus only two possibilities left. Before considering these we would like to ask the question : which of the two sexes is better equipped to shoulder the responsibilities of headship of the family ? Is the one equipped with rational qualities in a better position to head the family or that whose existence is characterised by emotions ? The problem is resolved the moment we realize that it is the man equipped as he is with rational qualities and a strong physical body who is more entitled to head than woman who is by her very nature emotional, susceptible to external influences and thus ill equipped for the struggle of life as well as the headship of the family. Even woman herself does not respect a man who is a weakling and can easily be conquered by her. She despises him ; nor can ever bring herself to trust him. This behaviour of woman may be the vestigial remnant of the attitude of mind she imbibed over the centuries and through the training she received in the past.

1. The Holy Quran (21 : 22)

The fact is however undeniable that she is still strongly drawn to a physically well built man, as is shown by the case of the American woman. Though she has achieved an equal footing with man and has come to be recognized as a quite independent being, she enjoys subjecting herself to man, makes love to him and tries to win him over. She is moved by his strong well-built body, broad chest and when satisfied of his strength as against her own physical weakness she surrenders her person to him.

Woman may seek after leadership in family life only so long as she has no children and has no worry to educate and train them. After having children she can ill afford to shoulder extra responsibilities, for her functions as a mother are already far too great a burden upon her.

This does not however mean that man should be a dictator over woman or in his house, for the leadership entails obligations and duties which can be discharged only through mutual consultation and co-operation. Success in management means a reciprocity of understanding and perpetual sympathy. Islam insists that love and mutual understanding and perpetual sympathy rather than conflict and competition should form the basis of family life.

Says the Holy Quran : " *Consort with them in kindness*,"
(4 : 19), and the Holy Prophet said : " *Best amongst
you is he who is good to his wife.*" (*Tirmizi*). The gauge
thus laid down by the Holy Prophet to judge a man is
his behaviour towards his wife. And a very sound
standard it is, for no man can ill treat his wife unless
he is spiritually diseased and absolutely lost to virtue
or at least partially handicapped.

But it is the " official " relationship within a
family that has occasioned many a doubt that call
for an explanation. Some of these doubts arise out
of woman's obligations towards man and some centre
around the problems of divorce and polygamy.

Let us remark here that marriage is primarily
a personal relationship and like every other relationship between two persons depends, in the first place,
on the personal, psychological, rational and physical
harmony between the persons concerned. The law
can hardly secure any of these by an order. Therefore
if a married couple live in perfect peace and harmony
it may not necessarily be due to their meticulous
observance of all the rules of matrimonial life. For,
many a time it happens that consummation of love
between man and wife followed their bitter bickerings.
Similarly if a state of discord and conflict is witnessed
in the married life of a couple it may not be due to

some mistake on the part of the husband or a gross disobedience of the wife. It is just possible that both of them may be exceptionally noble as human beings, but still their temperament may differ and so they may lament the impossibility of coming to terms between themselves but still they may not be able to effect a compromise with each other.

Despite all this the common law must however take note and frame rules for married life, for no system of life can claim comprehension if it does not provide for a law governing this delicate aspect of man's life. A law setting the general and inviolable limits at least must be there, with the man and woman to work out the details of it in the prescribed limits.

If there is love and peace between a couple, quite naturally they would not go to law as successful marriage seldom stands in need of the legal protection or verdict. But when there arises a conflict between them, they seek the aid of law in the hope that it would put an end to it.

Of law it is expected that it should be just ; should not favour one of the parties to the detriment of the other ; and should as far as possible cover the widest possible range of cases. At this place I must however repeat that no law can possibly cover all the different cases or situations cropping up in human life, nor is its rigid, literal application to all the cases considered just or a sound precept.

Let us cast a glance over the Islamic law with regard to the obligations of the wife in whose name all this hue and cry is being raised. With regard to her obligations prescribed in Islamic law, the following three points may be considered :

(1) Do these obligations constitute an injustice towards woman ?

(2) Are they unilateral and carry no rights with them ?

and (3) Are these obligations perpetual, such as woman can never free herself from ?

Woman has three most important obligations towards her husband : (1) she should obey him whenever he should want her to go to bed with him ; (2) should not allow anyone to defile the bed of her husband whose presence is resented by him ; and (3) should be faithful to him in his absence.

As to the first of these, a little explanation is necessary to appreciate it properly. Its wisdom is obvious. Man's physical constitution is such as impels him to seek sexual gratification more often so as to relieve himself of its oppression and so that he may be able to perform his duties in practical life more smoothly and efficiently. He is in his youth in particular far more dominated by the sex instinct and feels the need to gratify it more acutely than a woman does, although sexually she is far more profound than he, and is physically and psychologically more intensely inclined to it, but her inclination may not express itself in the physical sense alone. Marriage is a means to gratify this natural urge of man as well as meet the demands of his spiritual, psychological, social and economical life. Now the question is: what should a husband do if on approaching his wife he is coolly brushed off by her ? Should he seek to establish illicit relations with other women ? No society can approve of such a course, nor can the wife herself agree that her husband should be physically or psychologically attracted by another woman as no matter what the conditions of life be that would be too much for her.

As to the cause of the refusal of a wife to go to bed with her husband on his inviting her, there may again be three causes : (1) she hates him, and so feels disinclined to have sex relations with him ; (2) she loves her husband but hates the sexual act and hence refuses him — an abnormal state which nonetheless enjoys wide currency in practical life ; and (3) she is a loving wife, does not hate the sexual act but at that particular moment happens to be disinclined to it.

The first of these causes forebodes a permanent condition and may thus be not confined to a particular act or period of time. In such a situation marital bond cannot survive for long. The best thing to do in such a case would be to let the man and the wife separate from each other. The woman in a sense enjoys more facilities in this respect than a man does, as we shall shortly see.

In the second instance too the condition of the wife may bear a stamp of permanency. Its origin lies not in the sexual craving of the husband alone. It must be remedied satisfactorily and a complete harmony between the husband and the wife must be restored. Either the husband should check himself if his wife refuses him or the wife must comply with the wish of her husband like a truly loving wife as she would not like to get separated from him. Failing this they may be separated from each other in a very gentle manner. But so long as they live together as husband and wife, the wife must according to the Islamic law comply with the wish of her husband in sexual matters, as it is but natural. It does not necessarily imply an arbitrary authority or compulsion. It is meant to prevent the husband from being driven to pursue a course of moral perversion or entering into another marriage contract, a thing all the more painful to the wife. The law does not however insist on the continuance of such strained relations as make the wife feel repulsion from her husband and her love for him changes into a positive dislike due to his insistance on having his way in sexual matters. They may in this case too better separate from each other.

The third situation is a temporary condition and it may easily be remedied. Such an aversion to the sexual act may be the result of physical exhaustion, weariness or occupation as her psycho-physical disposition is quite capable of overcoming these in due course of time. This form of apathy in woman may be encountered by offering gifts to her and an ingenious love-play before the actual intercourse so as to transform it into a higher spiritual union rather than a purely animal and physical relationship that it might otherwise degenerate to. This love-play may also be helpful in removing the basic cause of aversion.

If on the other hand a wife desires sexual intercourse but the husband is for some reason disinclined to it — a rare phenomenon among men in their youth at least — the wife is not without means to induce her husband to resume sex-relationship with her. The very law that lays the wife under an obligation to comply with the wish of her husband also sees to it that she too should get her wishes met with. It prescribes that the husband must also fulfil his marital duties if and when his wife should so desire.

If the husband is unable to satisfy her, their marriage may dissolve. Thus we see that in the Islamic law both parties have got their duties as well as their rights. There is as such no compulsion or disregard of the wife implied in it.

The second obligation of the wife towards her husband that she should not allow any one such as is disliked by her husband to tread his bed, implies that she should not let anyone enter his house whom he would not like to enter into. (This does not however in any way refer to adultery as it is forbidden by law and will have to be eschewed even if the husband should happen to favour it). The wisdom of this commandment is manifest from the fact that a great many disputes between the married couples are caused by the intervention of a third person who spreads false reports, slanders and thus adds fuel to their family quarrels. What if in order to prevent such a development the husband were to demand of his wife not to allow a certain person into his house but she disregards it ? The result will be the presence of a constant source of mischief rendering the patch-up between them impossible. Thus this obligation of the wife also purports to the good of family life including the children who require a congenial atmosphere of love and sympathy for their proper and normal growth.

It may be asked : why then did the law not also provide that the husband too should be under an obligation not to allow anyone into his house if his wife should happen to disapprove of it ? In normal life when husband and wife are living in peace and love and are civilized enough no such question may arise at all, as they may feel no difficulty in reaching an understanding between themselves on all such points. But supposing that discord does creep in, straitening their relations and making it impossible for them to reach an agreement between themselves, they would have to go to court for a rapprochement of their differences. Now if the wife should enjoy the right to debar anyone from the house of her husband, it may make the matter worse, for we may at this place point out that the impressions of the woman are in most of the cases illogical as they are purely the reflection of her own peculiar personality rather than the outcome of any prudence. They may have sprung up from her constrained relations with the in-laws, the mother or the sister etc. of her husband. Therefore to make it incumbent upon the husband to obey his wife in such a circumstance would not be a judicious step ; it would rather be an act of mawkish tenderness that may soon suffer a change or be completely unfounded in reality.

By this I do not mean to say that the husband is always in the right in all that he does. It is just possible that his behaviour may under certain circumstances be puerile and shifty. Nor do I mean that the wife alone is always in the wrong. She may be quite justified in hating her husband who, it is just possible, may be the real cause of their constrained relations. But as the law is framed for the normal human life where man has been found to act more rationally than a normal woman does, it gives a degree of importance to man over woman. The wife is however free to secure a separation from her husband if she is convinced that she can no longer grin and bear with him.

The third obligation of the woman — the guarding of her husband's property and honour in his absence — is but a natural and logical sequence of marriage such as none may dare call in question. It is however not a unilateral obligation but rather a bilateral one : both husband and wife must remain faithful to each other.

Let us now take up the case of a wife and her husband one or the other of whom turns rebellious. The fact that man is in charge and the maintainer of the woman necessitates that he should have the right to admonish his disobedient wife as the following verse clearly shows : " *As for those (women) from whom ye fear rebellion, admonish them and banish them to beds apart, and scourge them. Then if they obey you, seek not a way against them.*" (4 : 34).

The reader must take note of the fact how this verse gradually proceeds with the description of the means of correcting one's wife ending with the chastisement. We admit that this privilege may be abused by some men but so can every other right. The only remedy for such a situation lies in the spiritual and moral elevation of people the importance of which Islam has never lost sight of. But the law laid down in the above verse seeks to preserve family life and safeguard it against disintegration. The law to be really useful or effective requires a power to deal with those who break it, for otherwise it is no more than an empty word ; it loses all its usefulness.

Marriage is an institution that aims at the common good of the married couple. It is supposed to realize the greatest possible good for all the concerned with the love and harmony that prevails at home without any intrusion from law. But in the event of a married couple's being at variance with each other the consequent ill-effect may not remain confined to their persons alone ; they may also adversely affect the children, the next generation.

Now if the wife is the cause of this trouble whom should we expect to correct her ? the court ? well, the court cannot but widen the gulf between husband and wife by interfering with their private affairs. Their differences may be trivial and temporary but the interference of the court may by airing them aggravate the situation. The pride of the parties may not allow them to patch up. Therefore it is only reasonable that the court should not busy itself with the trifles of conjugal life.. It may step in in the important matters only when all the other means to achieve an approchement have failed.

No sensible man can ever think of taking to court all his petty grievances that he daily suffers from almost every minute of his earthly existence. It would require setting up courts in almost every home to dispense with such grievances day and night.

It shows that there must of necessity be some local authority to deal with such cases as require admonition. It is this very local authority that is exercised by man as he is the real and ultimate head of his family. He is in the above verse enjoined upon to admonish his wife without injuring her self-respect. If she desists, the evil is mended. But if she persists in the wrong course he should banish her to a bed apart — a chastisement that is a bit severer than the first one. It also illustrates how penetrating an eye Islam has into the psychology of woman who being proud of her beauty and personal charm at times plays a coquette so much so that virtually it becomes an impudence. As such her separation to a bed apart means that the husband is impervious to her beauty, charm and coquetry. This may deflate a little her swollen pride and thus bring her back to her senses. But if all these means of correction fail to bring her round, the implication is that her impudence has advanced too far to be mended by anything save a very severe chastisement. Then it is that the husband is permitted to beat her as a last resort in his attempt to correct her conduct without intending to torment her. This is why the Islamic law has laid it down that the chastisement should be of a mild severity.

Does such rough treatment of woman degrade her and injure her self-respect ? It does not. For, to begin with we should remember that it is just a precautionary measure resorted to only when all the other conciliatory measures fail. Secondly, we must also bear in mind that in certain cases of psychological perversions chastisement is the only effective remedy. The science of psychology tells us that in normal cases the above mentioned conciliatory measures viz. admonishing and separating apart her bed etc. are quite effective but in acute cases e.g. masochism they fail, the only remedy in such cases being the physical chastisement of the persons concerned. Women rather than men are more generally the victim of this psychological malady. They derive pleasure from humiliation and sufferings. (Men are on the other hand commonly afflicted with " sadism " which is marked with a morbid love for cruelty). Now if the wife belongs under this class of women, clearly her correction can be effected through chastisement alone so that she might have her desired beating and then come to herself again. Strange though it may appear, it is a fact that sometimes a man suffering from sadism marries a masochistic woman and they live in perfect love and harmony notwithstanding the abnormal basis on which their union rests. Similarly the cases of a sadistic woman marrying a masochistic brand husband and then beating him frequently to his fill are not missing, though rare. The beating restores the balance of mind of the masochistic husband and so they live on in love and harmony. But if the situation is not so seriously aggravated the beating may not be needed at all, as that allowed by law is no more than a precautionary measure. One should not on every trivial disagreement rush in and start beating his wife. The description of the corrective measures one after the other in the above Quranic verse stresses the same fact. The Holy Prophet forbade men to exercise this right except in cases where they have no other course. Thus speaking in reproof of physical chastisement he said : " *Let none of you scourge his wife the scourge of a camel and then towards the end of the day have intercourse with her. (Bukhari).*"

If on the other hand the wife should fear ill treatment from her husband the law is a bit different : " *If a woman feareth ill treatment from her husband, or desertion, it is no sin for them twain if they make terms of peace with themselves. Peace is better."* The Holy Quran *(4 : 128).*

Some men may on this point be inclined to demand perfect equality between men and women. But the question is not one of a fanciful and theoretical justice but of that form of it which is practicable and in line with human nature. No woman would like to beat her husband in return for his beating her, neither in the "civilized" West nor in the "backward" East. She does not respect the husband whom she can beat and chastise. This is why no woman has yet demanded a right to beat her husband.

The important thing to take note of here is however that Islam does not necessitate that the woman should suffer ill treatment at the hands of her husband passively. She can in such a case secure a separation from him.

We have in the foregoing pages seen that :

(1) The obligations of a wife towards her husband are not enforced arbitrarily. They are meant for the general good of the society of which the wife forms but a part ;

(2) Most of her obligations are balanced with similar obligations which the husband has to discharge with respect to her. As to the few situations where man enjoys in one way or another a precedence

over the woman the basic consideration has been the difference between their respective dispositions. It does not at all spring from any desire to humiliate or disgrace the woman ;

(3) As against this authority given to man over the woman, the latter has the legal right to leave her husband if he should ill-treat her.

As to the separation which has been referred to above at more than one place and which provides woman with a practical way to get her marriage dissolved freeing herself of the obligations thereof, there are three ways to secure it :

(a) The woman may secure the right to divorce from her husband (at the time of entering into the marriage contract with him). The Islamic law explicitly allows it although few women do ever exercise it. Still the right is there which they may exercise whenever they should need it.

(b) Or she may demand a divorce from her husband on the plea that she hates him and can no longer live with him. I have heard that some courts do not enforce this principle and do not on her demanding it decree a woman's separation from her husband, although the principle is clearly laid down and supported by the personal example of the Holy Prophet and is thus a part of the Islamic law. The only condition for the woman in such a case is that she should give back to her husband the dowry she received from him — a perfectly just condition, for, the husband too in the event of divorcing his wife is obliged to forgo in her favour all that he might have given her. Thus in order to free themselves both, man and woman have to bear material loss in equal manner.

(c) The third course open before the wife is to secure divorce along with her dowries as well as the sustenance allowance provided she should be able to convince the court that her husband has ill-treated her or has failed to give her the sustenance allowance agreed upon by both of them and furnish the necessary proofs thereof. The court shall dissolve the marriage contract if it is convinced of the legitimacy of her claims.

These are the weapons which a woman may resort to if a situation should call for. They perfectly balance the authority man enjoys over her.

We have heard many a gloomy tale about the miseries caused by the divorce ; how the wife and the children suffered ; and how the courts are crowded due to the seemingly never ending family feuds arising from divorce. It often happens that a woman who is a happy and dutiful wife doing her best to upbring her suckling besides joyfully expecting yet another one, all of a sudden is approached by a messenger handing her over a bill of divroce from her husband which might have been occasioned by a sudden whim or desire of the husband. It is just possible that he has seen a woman whom he believes to be more beautiful and has taken fancy to her, or it may be that he is prompted by a wish to have a change in his sexual routine, or it may have just proceeded from the refusal of the wife to have intercourse with her husband due to her sluggishness and exhaustion.

Isn't it, they say, then desirable that this dangerous weapon with which man may in a fit of faithlessness toy so recklessly and wreck the life of a peaceful, patient woman besides darkening the future prospects of his young innocent children, should be taken away from him ?

As to these miseries we admit that divorce does lie at the root of all these, but what is the way out ? Should we abolish the right of the man to pronounce divorce ? If so, how are we to meet the painful situation that might as well result from such an abolition — a situation such as we meet with in the Roman Catholic countries where divorce is not permissible ? Is a home wherein the husband and the wife are constantly wrangling together and are averse to any fellowship with each other worth the name, especially, if the marriage be a perpetual bond and freedom from it impossible to secure ? Will such situation not be conducive to moral crimes ? The husband as well as the neglected wife might be driven to seek mistresses and friends outside home to gratify their sexual instinct. Surely the children cannot grow up properly and develop healthy sound personalities in such a dismal, cloudy and gloomy atmosphere, for the mental health of children and their sound development is dependent more on the social atmosphere they breathe in rather than a mere parental care. That is whence the abnormalities met with in people's lives spring. Their roots lie embedded in the life of their quarrelsome parents.

It is also suggested that the right of the man to divorce should be restricted, that is the divorce should not take effect on the mere pronouncement of it by the man. Only the court should have the authority to decree the divorce after appointing arbiters one each from among the people of the man and the woman. The arbiters should thoroughly discuss the problem, trying to make the husband desist from his intention and agree to make peace with his wife. If all their efforts fail, only then the divorce should be ordered by the court, not by the husband.

I wonder if there is any legal objection such as due to which the adoption of such a conciliatory measure to restore peace and harmony between the spouses may not be possible. But I do not think there is really any need for the court to step in as the remedy prescribed by the Islamic law is in itself quite sufficient for the purpose. Peace and harmony between the spouses depends more on themselves and their desire to mend than on anything else. If the will be there and both wish peace, the friends and kindred may prove as useful as any court ; if there is no will then not even the highest court in the world may succeed in restoring peace between them. There are the " civilized " nations among whom only a court may decree a divorce after admonishing the parties to exhort them to patch up relations, but still large numbers of divorces do take place there. In America alone the rate of divorce is 40% — the highest in the world.

As to the suggestion that divorce should take place only if the court is convinced that the fault lies with the wife and if the husband should prove that to live with her is a nuisance, we wonder what honour do these people want to bring to woman by making her live in the house where she is despised and where the husband ever reminds her that he no longer loves her. Should she even then stay on in his house in order to defraud him ? Surely the law cannot sanction such a conduct, nor is fraud the only course of action for her that she should have to live in that house as a despised and helpless wretch.

Should she then stay in the house of the father of her children to train and upbring her children ? But will it be desirable and in any way helpful in the proper upbringing of children if they live in such an atmosphere permeated with abominable injustice ?

The fact is that the solution of all these problems lies in the moral, cultural, psychological and spiritual training and education of society as a whole through a long process of intellectual purgation so as to make virtue and goodness prevail in the end providing a sound basis of social life. The husband will then realize that marital relations are very sacred and should not be disrupted in such an impetuous manner.

Such a process of moral and spiritual elevation is however a very long and slow process. It requires that the social life of the community should be regulated by the Islamic law with the help of an incessant struggle and co-operation of all the social institutions — home, school, film, radio, press, literature, religion and the general public to achieve this end. It is a long and arduous process yet is the only sure way to secure sound results.

As against this we must remember that the law is primarily concerned with administration of justice. It aims at giving both parties, the husband and the wife, their due share of it guaranteeing them the right to secure a separation in case they should find that they can no longer live with each other. In this connection, we must also remember that "*of all things allowed to men divorce is most hated by God.*" (*The Prophet*)

With regard to the institution of polygamy we should not lose sight of the fact that it is just an emergency law. It does not at all represent any fundamental principle of Islamic law : "*Marry of the women, who seem good to you, two or three or four ; and if ye fear that ye cannot do justice (to so many) then one (only).*" *The Holy Quran (4: 3)*

As pointed out in this verse what is required of men is justice which being difficult to achieve in polygamy, the injunction virtually comes to imply that men should contact with one wife only. Thus the Islamic law in normal life favours monogamy rather than polygamy. But there are certain circumstances under which monogamy becomes an unjust rather than a just institution. In such extraordinary circumstances Islamic law leaves the door open to polygamy, for although in it complete justice is impossible to attain, the disadvantages resulting therefrom are far less serious than those flowing from monogamy in such emergencies.

During the wars especially when a large number of men are decimated, balance between the sexes is seriously shaken. In such circumstances polygamy becomes a social necessity as it may save society from the sexual anarchy that generally follows the decimation of a large number of men with a corresponding rise in the number of women in society who have no male bread-winner. Such women may earn their living, but what about their sexual gratification ? This may make them fall an easy prey to the lust of men. But even after this, their most innate craving may still remain ungratified — their craving for children, without whom their whole existence is reduced to a dull, lifeless drudgery.

Should then in such circumstances the widowed women be left to gratify their sex urge as best as they can without having any consideration about the social morals ? The French nation suffered this fate. The whole social structure was as a result of it disintegrated ; and the French were jolted down from the exalted position they enjoyed in history. Such a social disintegration can be averted only if a man is explicitly permitted by law to have more than one woman at a time provided that he should treat all of them with justice in all things (save of course in the emotional attachment which is beyond man's control.)

In such other emergencies as the one met with during the wars the same need for polygamy is indicated. There may be some men who are over-active sexually. Such people can hardly be content with one wife, nor can they check their overflowing sexual energy. They should be permitted by law to have a second wife, for otherwise they may contract illicit sexual relations with girl friends, a situation that can hardly be tolerated by any healthy social set-up.

There are beside this certain other circumstances as well under which polygamy offers the only solution to many problems viz. sterility of wife or a chronic disease which renders the sexual union impossible. In the first case *i.e.* when the wife is sterile we may not blame her for it, but why should her husband be deprived of issue, love for which is the strongest in human heart ? The second marriage is the only sensible remedy in such a situation. The first wife may stay on with them or secure a separation. As to the chronically diseased wife let it not be said that sex is in itself a base instinct and therefore its gratification should not be sought after by undermining the happiness and well-being of an innocent woman. For, the problem here is not whether sex urge is base or exalted. It is rather of the practical need which none may afford to ignore. If the man

willingly forgoes his sexual pleasure and is mindful
of his wife's pleasure, it is most welcome as an act of
nobleness and generosity, on his part but God does
not burden anyone with more than he can easily
bear. Moreover to face the facts as they are is more
realistic and better than a spurious nobleness in the
guise of which all sorts of infamies are perpetrated
as is generally the case with a people amongst whom
polygamy is disallowed.

We must also in this connection bear in mind
the situations such as render a husband unable to
give love to his wife or divorce her. In this and all
kindred situations polygamy provides the only answer
and solution.

Now we propose to take up some other doubts
that are prevalent about the problem of woman.
To begin with is the right of the woman to work
and move in public, which is duly endorsed by Islam.
In the early period the woman worked outside whenever
there was any genuine need for it. Similarly Islam
did not forbid women to go out and work in such
social institutions as required their services *e.g.* female
education, nursing, medical treatment of women
etc. Their services may for these purposes be procured as those of men are procured in wars etc. If a
woman has no bread-winner she may as well go and

work outside. But it must be remembered that Islam permits women to go outside their houses only when there is really a genuine need for them to do so.

Otherwise it does not in principle approve of women's outside activities as the West and the communist nations do. This is a mere folly which Islam does not approve of, for a woman cannot participate in social activities but at the cost of her real primary function within her home by leaving which she may engender many psychological, social and moral problems.

That woman is physically, intellectually and intuitively best equipped for her real function of motherhood can hardly be disputed by anybody. Therefore if her attention is diverted to other unimportant activities, humanity is bound to suffer. In such a case she becomes just a plaything in the hands of men and a slave to their foolish demands, giving way to unchecked luxury and license. Islam cannot approve of this situation which if it did, it might be shorn of its chief distinctive mark of holding that mankind is a coherent entity that does not suffer a change with the changing circumstances.

It is also said : why can't a woman be a worker outside as well as a mother inside home at the same time with a nurse taking care of children in her absence ? This is a baseless assertion, for a nurse may give the children in the most efficient manner all possible physical, intellectual or psychological help but she cannot give them one thing — the love, the care of a mother and the mother herself — but for which life can hardly flourish or good manners take roots.

However hard they may try, the crazy standard bearers of civilization or the foolish votaries of communism can never effect any change in human nature. The child badly stands in need of the mother's attention during at least the first two years of its growth — full and undivided attention and love in which no partnership is tolerated even if the partner be the child's own dear brother. How can a nurse give this motherly care and love to children ? She has in most of the cases ten to twenty children to look after. The children cannot but quarrel together over their playthings and for the attention of the artificial mother they share in common. The quarrel thus comes to stay as a permanent feature of their lives leaving their hearts cold and hard without love, without any fraternal affection.

A nurse may be, if there is any genuine need for her, engaged to take care of the children. But without any such need resort to her is nothing short of foolishness.

The crazy westerners may however excuse themselves on the basis of their historical, geographical and politico-economic conditions of life, but what about us living in the Islamic East ? Have we too got any such excuse ? Are there no more male workers available to work outside so that we should require extra female workers ? or have the Muslim men, fathers, brothers, husbands or kinsmen abstained from supporting their daughters, sisters, wives or poor relations and left them to themselves to go out and scratch a living for themselves ?

It is also said that by working outside a woman may attain her independent economic existence which may enhance her honour and prestige in society. But we would like to know if Islam has denied an independent economic position to woman ? The fact is that the problem with which the Islamic world is faced today is not that of a system but it is poverty due to which both men and women have been deprived of all facilities of decent living. The solution lies in stepping up our material production so that the whole of the nation may prosper, men as well as women and so that none may remain poor. The competition between women and men over the possession of sources of economic production is no solution at all.

Some people also aver that by working outside a woman may help increase the income of her family, for the income of a single earning member cannot equal that of the two. This may be true in certain individual cases but if all women take to outside work, family life should be crippled leading to long separations of husband and wife which may result in moral crimes. What economic, social or moral justification is there to make the woman work outside at so enormous a price ?

Assigning the woman her natural function of nursing the human race wholeheartedly Islam had an eye to the demands of human nature as well as those of society. So man was charged with the duty of supporting her and providihg for her all her requirements so as to leave her free from all irrelevent worries, besides giving her the highest respect and regard so much that " *when a man enquired of the Holy Prophet :* " *Who has the first claim to my good treatment ?* " *he said* " *your mother.*" *The man said* " *And then who ?* " *the Prophet said :* " *Then your mother,*" *The man asked :* " *And then ?* " *again the Prophet replied :* " *Then your mother !* " *The man once again asked :* " *And then ?* " *The Prophet said :* " *Then your father !* " (*Muslim and Bukhari*).

What then is all this uproar by the Muslim woman of today about ? Is there any right or facility that

Islam has not already given her so that she should still feel constrained to launch a campaign to win them through means such as suffrage and representation in parliament ? Let us see :

She demands an equal human status. But Islam has already given this to her in theory as well as in practice before law.

She wants economic independence and the right to participate in social life directly. Well, Islam was the first religion that gave her this right.

She wants the right to education ? Islam not only recognizes it but makes the acquisition of it obligatory on her as well.

Does she want the right not to be given in marriage without her permission ? Islam has given her this right as well as the right to arrange her own marriage.

Does she demand that she should be treated kindly and fairly while performing her functions within the house ? and that she should have the right to ask for a separation from her husband if he should fail to treat her in a just and fair manner ? Islam does give her all these rights and makes it incumbent upon men to safeguard them.

Also does she want the right to go and work outside ? Islam recognizes this right of hers too.

Or does she seek the freedom to indulge in base, degrading and humiliating sybaritics ? Well, Islam cannot grant this to her as it does not also allow men to degrade themselves by indulging in such depravities. This license does not however hang on the representation of women in parliaments. They may do well to wait patiently till the social relationships and traditions disintegrate and degenerate to anarchy. Then all those craving for this license may enjoy it unchecked.

There are certain other people who maintain that though our conditions and values of life differ from those of the West, yet practically the position of woman in the East is so low that one cannot but protest against it. Her western counterpart has already won her freedom besides a high social status, so why should not the eastern woman as well, following in the footsteps of her western sister, endeavour to get back her usurped rights ?

This is no doubt true. The woman in the Islamic countries is generally backward with neither respect nor any grace. She lives a life similar to that of animals ; her whole existence is but another name for mean earthly desires ; she suffers privations more than she ever tastes of happiness; she is made to surrender more than she is given ; and seldom rises above the level of a purely impulsive existence.

This is also true, but may we ask : who is responsible for this state of affairs ? Does Islam or its teachings have anything to do with it ?

The fact is that the miserable plight of the eastern woman is the result of the economical, social, political and psychological conditions prevailing in the East today. We must take note of these if we really want to reform our social life and know as to where these evils spring from.

At the root of the present miserable plight of the eastern woman lies the wretched poverty that the East has been afflicted with now for many a generation past. It is the social injustice which makes a group of people live in luxury and profusion whereas their fellowbeings do not find enough to feed or clothe themselves properly and the political repression which splits a people into rulers and ruled, the former enjoying all privileges without the attendant obligations, and the latter labouring under heavy burdens with no rights or compensations in return. The dark clouds of oppression that overcast the heavens above are the result of these very social factors. It is these circumstances that are in effect responsible for the present humiliation and persecution of woman in the East.

Woman craves for an amicable relationship of love and mutual respect between her and her companion, man. But how can this love and respect find expression in this suffocating atmosphere of bleak poverty and social repression ? For, not only woman but man too is the victim of these circumstances although he may seem to be comparatively better off than her.

Man treats woman roughly and persecutes her as a reaction to that harsh and rough treatment and persecution that he himself suffers at the hands of the people around him. He is disgraced and his self pride is wounded by the rough treatment of the chiefs of the villages, the police officers, and factory owner or the head of the state. He meets nothing but disgrace and humiliation in social life but he cannot avenge himself upon all these antagonistic forces, so he comes back to his house and gives vent to his anger on his wife and children or those who happen to be near him at the time.

It is this accursed poverty that exhausts man to the utmost limit, totally incapacitating him for love, sympathy or forbearance towards those with whom he comes into contact. Again it is this very wretched poverty that makes woman put up patiently with tyranny, cruelty and rough treatment from her husband for she knows that life without a bread-winner would be even worse. She dare not even claim her legal rights fearing that her husband taking it ill might divorce her. And what would she do if he divorced her? Who will support her ? For, her parents are themselves too poor to support her. They cannot but advise her to return to her husband and bear up with the degradation and humiliation as best as she can. This is one reason why woman is so degraded and humiliated in the East today.

Secondly, backward as it is today the East lacks ideals as well as self consciousness and is plunged into a dark night of ignorance. It has become devoid of all higher values of humanity save one — power and its various manifestations which it worships and holds weakness to be in itself a sufficient justification to despise or hold in contempt anyone bearing its stamp.

It is this self same worship of power that makes man, the sterner sex, hate weak woman. He finds it hard to honour or respect woman as a human being, for he also lacks the moral refinement so necessary for such an attitude toward the weaker sex. A woman may however be honoured if she happens to possess wealth, the key to power and authority over others.

Similarly in a backward society such as the East at present the people sink low to the level of a purely or nearly instinctive existence. They are sex-ridden and sex colours all their views and attitudes towards life. As such they come to view woman as a means of pleasing and gratifying their lust and nothing else.[1] She loses all respect as a human being as psychologically, intellectually and spiritually she is held to be too much below man to deserve or claim it. As a result thereof the sexual union of men and women is reduced to a purely animal act where the male always dominates the female — its two distinctive marks being consciousness of the male at the time of the act of the dominance of the female over him, and ignoring her later on.

Afflicted as it always is with ignorance and hunger, a backward community can hardly afford to spare time or energy to achieve moral elevation and discipline, although it is through these alone that a people can attain to higher planes of humanity and rise above the plane of a purely animal existence. In the absence of such a moral and spiritual discipline or in the presence of the one that is unsuitable the inevitable result is that human life assumes a purely economic character, power is worshipped and life is measured in terms of animal passions.

It is in such a backward society that while performing her duties as a mother the woman unknowingly distorts the view of man towards woman. She turns her small child out as a petty dictator who

---

(I) So does the woman come to think of man with the only difference that because of his superiority as the incharge of the home and his earning capacity he enjoys a lion's share of sexual pleasure.

is wont to command an immediate obedience. She is too indulgent a mother to lay a reasonable check on the unreasonable demands of her boy. She tries to please him no matter how unreasonable or absurd his demands are. As a result of this over-indulgence he grows up as a man solely slave to his animal passions expecting others to obey him without a demur. But when in practical life his desires are thwarted he starts venting his rancour on people, men, women, and children around him.

These are the most important factors responsible for the disturbance and trouble witnessed in the East today. But for these, the woman in the East would not have suffered so much, nor occupied so low a position. Neither of these bears any relation to Islam ; they are incompatible with the true Islamic spirit.

Poverty ? Is it the result of Islam ? Certainly no, for it was but Islam that had made the community so rich that as happened in the days of Umar bin Abdul Aziz there remained not even a single man in it who was poor enough to deserve or receive alms. Islam is a practical system of life that brought about that great economic miracle in terms of practical life. It is this same system that we do earnestly seek to re-establish today. Islam as a system of life manages to get the wealth of the people distributed in a just and fair manner among the members of the community " *in order that it may not (merely) make a circuit between the wealthy among you.*"[1] It does not extol or approve of poverty ; rather it would see it abolished. Nor does it favour luxury and license ; it prohibits them both.

Poverty is the most important factor responsible for the troubles of the eastern woman of today. Once it is done away with, the greatest of woman's problems will be resolved forthwith. With that she will also get back her respect, for which purpose she may not necessarily have to go and work outside (though she has the right to do so) as she too will then have her share through inheritance in the increased wealth of the community which she may spend on her personal comfort only. When rich she may be sure to command the respect of men and be bold enough to exercise her rights without any fear or threat of poverty.

And what about the political injustice man is suffering from making him vent his repressed rancour on his wife at home? Is Islam responsible for that ?

Islam cannot be blamed for it either, as it preaches revolt rather than obedience to injustice. In this respect it so equitably regulated the relations of the rulers and the ruled that when once Omar said :

1. Thd Holy Quran (59 : 7)

" Hear and obey " a man from amongst the assembly of the believers retorted : " we shall not hear you, nor obey you, unless you tell us wherefrom have you got this sheet of cloth you are putting on ?" At this Omar did not fly into a rage. He on the other hand praised the man and clarified his position before the assembly, so that at last the man again got up and said : " Now give us your orders. We shall hear and obey you." It is precisely this form of government we seek to establish today, so that no ruler may dare oppress people ; so that the people may feel bold enough to speak their mind before rulers ; and so that the relations of a man with his wife and children are based on justice, charity, love and fraternity.

And the degeneration of higher human values, is Islam to be blamed for it ?

No, Islam has nothing to do with this degeneration of moral values. It seeks to elevate human beings inculcating in them higher spiritual values. It taught men that " *the noblest of you in the sight of Allah is the best in conduct,*" rather than the one who is the richest, mightiest, or strongest. Once these higher values are firmly established in society, the woman will no longer be looked down upon because of her weakness. The guage of a man's humanity in such a society is his fair treatment of his wife as the Holy Prophet said : " *The best amongst you is he who is best to his wife and I am the best amongst you as regards the treatment of my wife.''* Deep insight into the human psychology as this saying of the Prophet does exhibit, it also tells us that a man cannot ill-treat his wife without being a victim of psychological complexes and disorders or falling short of the true human standard.

And the degradation of men to a purely animal instinctive level of existence, is Islam the cause of it ? Surely no, Islam is not the cause of this degradation, for did it ever sanction that men should sink low to such an animal level ? Far from it, it seeks to elevate men and women to such a high plane of being that they are no longer mere slaves to their instincts, nor is their outlook upon life solely moulded by these. The sex relations of men and women are in the sight of Islam not purely animal relations. They rather represent their physical need which it approves of with an eye to free them from the over-domination of sex which if left to itself may thwart their creative pursuits belonging under the different realms of practice, science, arts or worship and which may in the absence of a lawful outlet drive them to adopt wrongful practices. As such though Islam does not condemn sexual relations of men and women, yet it does not approve of their being wholly taken up with them. It rather urges them to devote their energies to the higher and nobler ends of life, man exerting himself in the way of God incessantly and woman doing her best in training her children and looking after her household duties. Thus Islam gives both man and woman ideals that elevate them far above the purely animal level of needs and passions.

Or is the defective moral discipline the outcome of the impact of Islam ? The answer is a big no, for the Quran, the sayings of the Prophet are all full of moral precepts that aim at the spiritual elevation of human soul disciplining it to exercise self-control and observe the principles of justice and a respect for others such as one would himself expect from others.

Are then our traditions of social life really responsible for the backwardness of the women in the East? Are they in effect that have made her live like animals, inert, narrow-minded, ignorant, as some writers would have us believe ? The answer is again an emphatic no. Our past traditions do not forbid us to acquire knowledge, to work, or co-operate with others in social life, provided it aims at the well-being of the community and entails no adverse effects for it.

What these traditions[1] do not approve of are such foolish and unhealthy activities as the going out of

_____

(1) By " Traditions " we mean the true and genuine Islamic traditions and not those transplanted from foreign nations but the writers who launch their attacks against traditions do not differentiate between these two kinds.

women and walking openly and without any genuine need on the highways and roads. Surely none can dare say that the women can realize their potentiality and respect through these silly activities alone. They may in such situations fall an easy prey to the lust of the sybarite men as the experience of the enlightened, civilized western society girls does illustrate. As such the people opposing traditions seem to do so just because these do not see eye to eye with the self indulgence, license and luxury they so earnestly crave for.

There was in Egypt a non-Muslim writer who never lost an opportunity to disparage Islam overtly or covertly in his weekly magazine. He kept on reminding women : "Shake off your weatherworn traditions; come out of your houses and mix up with men courageously, by rushing in to take up work in factories and shops, not because there is any genuine need for it but just to get rid of your responsibilities as mothers and nurses of human race." He also said that the woman walked in the streets with her eyes down because she lacked courage and self confidence and was overwhelmed by fear of men. But when she through her experience achieves enlightenment she will be able to face men courageously.[1] He over-

---

(I)   The writer referred to above is Salama Musa. In whatever he penned his first care was to see that it in some way or other disparaged Islam, as did another Christian writer, Jurji Zaidan. Both of them formed the vanguard of the enemy who is at present as active against Islam as ever before.

looked the history which tells us that Ayesha who actively took part in the politics of her time and led armies into the battlefield used to talk to men from behind a veil. Moreover he also forgot to mention that the lowering down of eyes was not something peculiar to women alone, for history also tells us that the Holy Prophet Muhammad (peace be on him) was more modest than even the virgin maids. Did he also not possess self confidence ? or did he lack the consciousness of being a messenger of God ? How long will these writers keep on repeating and saying such silly things ?

That the woman is reduced to a very low plane of existence is undoubtedly true but the way to reform this situation is not that adopted by the woman in the West who was faced with peculiar circumstances and therefore was subject to typical aberrations of her own springing up from those circumstances.

Islam and Islam alone does provide a solution to the problem of woman no less than that of man. Let all of us, men, women, young and old turn towards it , strive hard to re-establish an Islamic state ; and enforce Islamic law in our lives. Only then shall we be able to realize in practice our beliefs and ideals. This is the only way to achieve symmetry and harmony in our life without any resort to injustice or tyranny.

ISLAM AND THE CONCEPT OF
PUNISHMENT

Some people often say, " Can we apply today the same barbarous punishments which were applied long ago in the desert ? Is it permissible to cut a thief's hand for five shillings ? Could such things take place in the twentieth century, which regards the criminal as the victim of society and maintains that he is entitled to medical treatment rather than punishment?" How is it that the twentieth century permits the slaughter of forty thousand innocent people in North Africa but forbids the rightful punishment of one single criminal ! !

Woe to people from deceptive words that often hide the truth ! !

So much for the twentieth century civilisation and its evils. Let us discuss the concept of crime and punishment in Islam.

Crime is often regarded as an individual aggression against the community. That is why the concept of crime and punishment is closely connected with a nation's concept of the individual — community relationship.

Individualistic countries — such as the capitalist western states — go too far in sanctifying the individual ; they regard him as the centre of all social life. Such countries straiten the state's right to restrict the freedom of the individual. This attitude is reflected in their conception of crime and punishment. They sympathize with criminals and treat them kindly because they are victims of corrupted circumstances, psychological complexes and nervous disorders which they could not overcome. Therefore, such states are inclined to reduce penalties until — especially in moral offences — they are no longer regarded as punishment.

At this stage psycho-analysis comes in to justify or explain away the crime. It will be noted that Freud was the champion of the historical change which regarded a criminal as the victim of the sexual complexes resulting from the repression of the sexual instincts by society, religion, morality and tradition. Later all schools of psychoanalysts followed Freud's example but many of them did not agree with him that the sexual energy was the centre of life. All such schools regard a criminal as a passive creature who is the victim of general and personal circumstances amidst which he was brought up. They believe in what is called " psychological determinism " that is to say, a man has no freedom of will or action with respect to the psychological energy which acts according to a predetermined manner.

On the other hand communist countries maintain that the community is a sacred entity against which the individual must not rebel. Therefore, such states inflict great penalties including death and torture on individuals who rebel against the state.

Communism refers offences to economic rather than psychological considerations — as Freud and other psychologists did. Communism holds that a society which suffers from economic disorder cannot foster virtues. Therefore, criminals should not be punished. But can the communists explain why crimes are still committed, why prisons and courts are still in use in Russia where the economy is governed by the theory of absolute equality ?

There is no doubt that both individualistic and communist conceptions are partly true. It is true that circumstances surrounding an individual have a great effect on his constitution and that the subconscious complexes may sometimes lead to crime. But man is not a completely passive being in confronting such circumstances. The psychoanalysts commit this mistake : they concentrate on the dynamic energy in man but they ignore the controlling energy which is quite inherent in the human system. The energy which enables a child to control his secretive glands and avoid wetting his bed after a certain age — is the same energy which can control his emotions and actions so that he may not continuously give in to his unruly passions and sudden whims.

On the other hand economic conditions do have some effect on the feelings and actions of individuals. It is true that hunger, by disintegrating the spirit and breeding hatred may lead to crime or moral corruption. But to say that only the economic factor does influence human conduct is a half truth. It is belied by the facts of life in the Soviet Union which claims to have wiped out hunger and poverty.

The main question is this : before deciding whether or not a criminal should be punished, we must determine the extent of his responsibility for the offence he committed. It is to be noted that Islam takes this into account when it considers the question of crime and punishment.

Islam never prescribes punishments haphazardly nor does it execute them without due consideration. In this respect Islam has a unique theory which combines the best of both worlds : the communist as well as the individualistic theories. Islam holds the balance of justice in the right manner and insists on examining all conditions and circumstances connected with the offence. On studying a crime Islam takes into account two considerations at the same time : the viewpoint of the criminal and that of the community against which aggression took place. In the light of such considerations Islam prescribes the fair punishment which is in accordance with the dictates of sound logic and wise reasoning and which must not be affected by delinquent theories and national or individual whims.

Islam imposes preventive punishments which may appear cruel or coarse if viewed superficially or without proper consideration. But Islam does not execute such punishments unless it ascertains that the crime was not justifiable or that the criminal was not acting under any obligation.

Islam prescribes that a thief's hand should be cut, but such punishment is never inflicted where there is the slightest doubt that the thief was impelled to crime by hunger.

Islam prescribes that both adulterer and adulteress should be stoned but it does not inflict such punishment unless they are married persons and upon conclusive evidence by four eye witnesses *i.e.* when two married persons flagrantly commit such a heinous crime.

It is to be mentioned that Islam took similar precautions with respect to all the punishments it had prescribed.

This is evident from a rule laid down by the third Caliph, Omar Ibn Alkhattab who is considered as one of the most prominent legislators of Islam. Omar was known for his strict rigidity in enforcing the rules of Alsharia (law) ; therefore it cannot be said that he was lenient in the interpretation of the law. It should be remembered that Omar did not carry out the punishment prescribed for theft (cutting the hand) during the year of famine when there was some doubt that people might be impelled to theft by hunger.

The above mentioned rule is best illustrated by the following episode :

> *" It was reported to Omar that some boys in the service of Hatib Ibn Abi Balta'a had stolen the she-camel of a man from the tribe of Muznah. When Omar questioned the boys they admitted the theft so he ordered their hands to be cut. But on second thoughts he said, " By God I would cut their hands if I did not know that you employ these boys and starve them so that they would be permitted to eat that which is prohibited unto them ". Then he addressed their employer saying : " By God, since I have not cut their hands I am going to penalise you with a fine that shall pain you " and he ordered him to pay double the price of the she-camel.*

This episode illustrates a very clear and express principle : punishment will not be inflicted where there are circumstances which impelled the wrong doer to commit the crime. This principle is supported by the saying of the Prophet : *" Avoid the execution of punishment by doubt."*

— 249 —

If we study the policy adopted by Islam in prescribing punishment we shall realise that Islam tries in the first place to purify society from circumstances that may lead to crime. After taking such precaution Islam prescribes a preventive and just punishment which may be inflicted upon persons who have no reasonable justification for their crimes. Where the community is unable to preclude circumstances which may lead to crime or where there is some doubt regarding the crime, the punishment will not be inflicted and the ruler will set the criminal free or he may inflict on him a light punishment (beating or imprisonment) in proportion to his extent of responsibility for the crime.

Islam strives by various means to preclude circumstances that may lead to crime. It strives to ensure a fair distribution of wealth. It even managed to wipe out all poverty in the regime of Omar bin Abdul Aziz. The Islamic state is responsible for the support of every citizen, regardless of his religion, race, language, colour or social status. The state is also responsible for ensuring decent work for all citizens. Where work is not available or if an individual is incapable of working, aid will be given to him from the public treasury.

Islam precludes all possible motives for robbery yet it examines all circumstances of a crime to ascertain before the infliction of the punishment, that the criminal was not impelled to commit crime.

Islam recognizes the strength and importunity of sex but it tries to satisfy the sexual instinct through legal means *i.e.* marriage. Therefore, Islam advocates early marriage and provides aid from the Public Treasury for those who wish to get married yet cannot afford to do so. On the other hand Islam purifies society from temptations which excite the passions. It also prescribes lofty and noble ideals which exhaust excessive vitality and direct it into the service of the public interest. It prefers that leisure time should be spent in trying to become closer and closer to God. In this manner Islam eradicates all motives that may lead to crime. Nevertheless, Islam does not hasten to inflict punishment unless the criminal has disregarded traditions and degenerated to animality by committing adultery so openly that he could be seen by four eye-witnesses.

It may be said that the present economic, social and moral conditions make it difficult for young men to get married and consequently they are led to adultery. There is some truth in that. But when Islam is truly applied there will be no maddening crazy temptations which lead young men to corruption, and there will be no pornographic motion pictures, newspapers or songs. No exciting tempatation will be walking along the streets. There will be no poverty which prevents people from marriage. It is then and only then that people may be called on to be virtuous and they can be virtuous. In such case punishment may be inflicted on offenders because they have no excuse or justification.

Before prescribing punishment, Islam tries in the first place to wipe out all circumstances and motives that may lead to crime. But even if after that a crime is committed Islam tries to waive the execution of punishment if there is any doubt about it. Could any other system match the justice of Islam ?

It is because some Europeans have not studied the reality of the Islamic concept of crime and punishment that they consider the punishments prescribed by Islam as barbarous and degrading to human dignity. They wrongly imagine that such punishments — like the European Civil punishments — will be inflicted every day. They also fancy that the Islamic society indulges in daily executions of flogging, hand-cutting and stoning. But the fact is that such deterrent punishments have been executed very rarely. The fact that the punishment for theft has been executed only six times throughout a period of four hundred years is a clear evidence that such punishment was primarily meant to prevent crime.

It should be remembered that Islam, before prescribing punishments aims at the prevention of crimes. Even in the very rare cases when such punishments were inflicted we may be sure that they were quite just.

There can be no reason why some Europeans are afraid of the application of the rules of Islam except that they are criminal by nature and persist in committing crimes which lack all justification.

On the other hand some persons imagine that such punishments have no practical significance. This is not true. These punishments were prescribed in order to frighten those individuals who have no reasonable motive for crime yet feel a strong desire for committing crimes. However strong their motives may be, the punishment will surely make them think twice before committing any crime. It is true that some young men may suffer from sexual repression. But so long as the community works for the public good and cares for all its members, the community is entitled to full security with respect to persons and property.

On the other hand, those people who tend to commit crimes for no clear reason are not left to their fate ; Islam tries all possible means to treat and restore them to normality.

It is to be regretted that some cultured youths and modern jurisprudents attack the punishments prescribed by Islam simply because they are afraid of being accused of barbarism by Europeans. But I am sure that such people would benefit very much by truly studying the wisdom of the Islamic legislation.

ISLAM AND CIVILIZATION

" Do you want us to go back to the age when people lived in tents — a thousand years ago ? Islam was allright for those savage and uncouth Bedouins of the desert, for it was simple enough to appeal to and attract them. But will a civilization based on the concept of God be of any use in the world of today, the age of supersonic planes, hydrogen bombs and movie cinemas. It cannot keep up pace with the advanced civilization of today, for it is static and therefore we have no other course but to shake it off if we are to become truly civilized and advanced like the rest of the world."

I was reminded of the doubts such as mentioned above when sometime back I came across an " educated " English man, who had been for the last two years stationed in Egypt.[1] He was a member of a group of U.N.O. experts that had been sent to Egypt to help the Egyptian Government raise the standard of living of the Egyptian peasants. But as despite all their " love " for the people of this region they did not know or care to learn their language, so the Egyptian Government assigned me the task to act

---

1) This book first appeared in Arabic in Egypt in 1955.

as an interpreter between them and the local peasants. Thus I came across the " educated " Englishman.

At the very outset I told him frankly that we, Egyptians hated them and would continue hating them so long as they continue commiting aggression in any part of the East. I told him that we also hated their allies, the Americans and others, for their unjust attitude towards Egypt, Palestine etc. Taken aback he looked at me for a while and then said :

" *Are you a communist ?* "

I told him that I was not a communist but a Muslim, who believed that Islam had a far superior civilization to their capitalist civilization as well as the communist one and that Islam was the most excellent system yet tried by mankind as it embraced the whole of man's life and struck a reasonable balance between different aspects of his existence.

Thus we continued talking together for about three hours at the end of which he said : " May be that what you tell me about Islam is correct but I for one would not deprive myself of the fruits of the modern civilization. I like travelling in planes and enjoy listening to the charming music on the radio. I would not like to forego all these pleasures."

Deeply surprised at his answer I said : " But who forbids you all these pleasures ? "

" Doesn't accepting Islam mean to go back to the age of barbarism and life in tents ?"

It is strange indeed that doubts such as these are continually cast against Islam although there is no reasonable basis for their existence as those who have gone through the history of this religion shall bear witness. Never even for a single moment did Islam stand in the way of civilization and progress.

Islam was revealed to a people composed mostly of bedouins who were so rough and cruel-hearted that the Quran said of them : " *The Bedouins are more hypocritical and Godless.*"

One of the great miracles of Islam is that it succeeded in changing such rough and coarse bedouins into a nation of human beings. Not only were they guided to the right path and elevated from animality to the loftier spheres of humanity, but they also became guides who directed humanity to the path of God. This is a clear illustration of Islam's miraculous ability to civilize people and refine souls.

There is no doubt that the refinement of the soul is in itself a noble end, worthy of human aspiration and striving ; it is one of the ultimate goals of civilization. But Islam was not contented with mere refinement. It always adopted all the manifestations of civilization which capture popular interest nowadays and which are regarded by some as the core of life. Islam patronized and fostered the civilizations of all the countries it conquered so long as such civilizations were not contrary to monotheism and did not divert people from doing good actions.

Islam also patronized and fostered the Greek scientific heritage including medicine, astrology, mathematics, physics, chemistry and philosophy. Islam continued to add new scientific achievements which bear witness that Muslims were deeply and seriously interested in scientific research. It was on the cream of the Islamic scientific achievements of Andalusia that the European Renaissance and its modern scientific inventions were based.

Now, when did Islam oppose a civilization which serves humanity ?

What is Islam's attitude towards the Western civilization of today ?

The attitude of Islam towards the present western civilization is the same as that it manifested towards every past civilization. Islam accepts all the goodness that such civilizations can yield but at the same time it rejects their evils. Islam has never advocated any policy of scientific or materialistic isolationism. It does not fight against other civilizations for personal or racial considerations because it believes in the

unity of humanity and the closeness of the relationship among people of different races and inclinations.

It should be known that the Islamic cause does
not oppose modern inventions nor do Muslims require that the appliances and tools should bear the
inscription : *In the name of God the Beneficent, the
Merciful* " before they agree to use such tools and
appliances at their homes, factories and farms etc.
It is quite sufficient if such tools and appliances should
be used in the name of God and for His sake. After
all, tools and appliances do not have any religion or
home-land, but the way of their use affects all the
people on earth. A gun, for example, is an invention
which has no religion, colour or homeland but you
will not be a Muslim if you use it in committing
aggression against others. Islam requires that a gun
shall only be used in repulsing aggression or in spreading the word of God throughout the world.

The motion picture is a modern invention too.
You can be a good Muslim if you use it in portraying
clean emotions, noble characters or depicting the
conflict among people for the sake of goodness. But
you will not be a Muslim when you use it in exhibiting
pornography, unrully passions or corrupted people
wallowing in all kinds of vice - moral, intellectual
or spiritual. Such motion pictures are bad and trivial
not only because they excite the lower instincts of
man but because they also represent life as cheap

and trivial existence restricted to trivial and cheap ends which can never be a proper spiritual food for humanity.

The Islamic faith has never opposed the adoption of scientific inventions achieved by humanity at large. Muslims should make use of all good scientific achievements. The Prophet says, "*The study of science is an ordinance.*" It is needless to say that the study of science, as used above, includes all kinds of knowledge. The Prophet called on people to study all branches of knowledge everywhere.

In conclusion it will be said that Islam does not oppose civilization as long as it serves humanity. But if a civilization consists of alcoholic liquor drinking, gambling, moral prostitution, colonialism and enslaving people under different names, Islam will fight against such so-called civilization and will do its best to protect humanity from succumbing to its temptations.

ISLAM AND REACTIONARISM

It is often alleged by some misguided people that some aspects of the Islamic way of life are no longer acceptable to people nor in line with the requirements of modern life. They add that some Islamic traditions were originally laid down for past generations and therefore have exhausted their ends and have become reactionary restrictions which obstruct and delay progress.

They would frequently ask such questions:

" Do you still insist on prohibiting usury which is an indispensable economic necessity of modern times ?

" Do you still insist on collecting Azzakat and distributing it in the same town where it is collected ? Azzakat is a primitive procedure which is incompatible with the modern system of government; besides, Azzakat humiliates the poorer inhabitants of a town or village by making them feel that they are the recipients of charity from the richer citizens."

"Do you still insist on prohibiting liquor drinking, gambling, free association of the sexes, dancing and having mistresses and lovers — all of which are indispensable social necessities which must be adopted as part of the general progress and development ? "

It is true that Islam prohibits usury but it is not true that usury is an economic necessity. In modern times there have been two economic systems which do not permit usury. Both Islam and communism, however different they may be in other respects, prohibit usury. Communism managed to find the necessary power for enforcing its doctrines, but Islam has not yet mustered its forces. But the present circumstances indicate that Islam is on the path to power and revival.

When the rule of Islam is established, the economic system will be based on foundations other than usury which will not be an economic necessity. Similarly, communist Russia laid down its economics on a basis which excludes usury.

There is no doubt that usury is not an indispensable economic necessity in modern times. It may be necessary for the capitalist world, because capitalists cannot exist without it. Nevertheless, leading Western economists do not approve of usury and warn that it will inevitably lead to the accumulation of wealth in the hands of few people. The masses will be gradually deprived of wealth and consequently they will be enslaved by the richer people. Western capitalism could supply us with many examples which prove these facts. It is to be remembered that Islam prohibited usury and monopoly, the two pillars of capitalism about one thousand years before the existence of capitalism. Islam was revealed by God Almighty Who can review all generations at one time, and Who knows what evils, economic catastrophes and feuds will be brought about by usury.

Usury may be a humiliating necessity where economy is dependent on foreign aid. But when our Islamic economy is independent and well established, our foreign relations will be based on free mutual reciprocity but not on subjection. In such case our economy will be guided by Islamic principles which prohibit usury. The rest of the world will then look to us as a developing and progressive force.

As for Azzakat, it was previously pointed out that it is not a charity donated to the poor but an ordinance prescribed by God as well as a right entrusted to the State.

In this chapter we shall deal with the accusation brought against Islam on account of the local character of Azzakat *i.e.* its distribution in the village where it is collected.

It is to be regretted that many intellectuals will greatly acclaim and welcome any western imported system and treat it as the pinnacle of civilization but when the same system is advocated by Islam it is regarded as a symbol of backwardness and reactionarism.

It may be useful to remind such " intellectuals " that the administrative system in U.S.A. is based on absolute decentralisation. The village or town is an independent economic, political and social unit within the general framework of the state as well as the United States. Now, the municipal council of each independent unit imposes certain taxes which are collected from the people of the unit and expended on the educational, medical, transport, or social services of the same town or village. If the revenues are more than the expenditure, the balance will be sent to the authorities of the city or to the state. On the other hand if revenues are less than expenditure the balance will be paid by the state. There is no doubt that this is an excellent administrative system which organises the efforts and does not burden the central government with all the services. On the other hand central authorities cannot understand the requirements of smaller units in the same way as the local authorities do.

Our intellectuals express their great admiration for such a system. They forget that the very system had been established by Islam thirteen hundred years ago. Taxes were collected by the local authorities of each village and were spent on the fulfillment of local needs. The balance between revenues and expenditure will be sent to or borrowed from the central Public Treasury.

As for the distribution of Azzakat, it was previously explained that nothing in Islam provides that it should be distributed to the recipients in cash or in kind only. It may be distributed to the poor in the form of educational, medical and social services or by direct support of those who cannot work owing to old age, weakness or infancy.

If we apply the rules of Islam to our present society we shall have to do no more than to establish smaller units which look after their own local affairs within the framework of the regional centres : the state, the Islamic world and all the world.

As for gambling, liquor and free association of the sexes — these are prohibited by Islam regardless of the silly attacks of the so called "progressive" pioneers. It might be significant to remember that even in France which is wholly addicted to liquor, a lady member of the National Assembly has recently tabled a motion for the prohibition of liquor.

Addiction to liquor is a symptom of social or individual malady. Liquor and other narcotics are needed only by delinquent societies where the differences among classes are so great that some people live in licentious luxury which deadens their senses while others live in utter deprivation which drives them to seek an escape from reality, and live in a world of their own invention. Narcotics and liquor may also spread in societies dominated by oppression, tyranny or in societies where the freedom of thought is subjected to many restrictions, or where people are obesessed by the struggle for earning a living, or where people suffer from the hateful and monstrous noise of modern machinery.

But this does not imply that such social maladies justify addiction to liquor. Addiction to liquor is a symptom of the malady. It is only logical that the social malady should be treated before prohibiting liquor. That is exactly what Islam did. It wiped out all the maladies and causes which drove people to liquor-addiction; then and only then it prohibited liquor drinking. Instead of criticizing Islam, the modern western civilization should rather learn from Islam how spiritual maladies are treated by economic, social, political, intellectual and physical reorientation.

As for gambling we need not dwell at great length upon pointing out that only trivial-minded people would approve it.

Now let us discuss the question of the association of the sexes — which has become the centre of great arguments.

Many superficial minded people accuse Islam of reactionarism on account of the restrictions it imposed on the association of the sexes. They express great admiration of the French civilisation which permits a pair of lovers to hold each other in public places and to forget all that is around, when they are enraptured in a wonderful kiss. No one would trouble them even the policeman would stand by to protect them from passers by. Woe to those who resent such a scene because they themselves will be despised !

Some others express great admiration for the American way of life. There, they say, the people are quite frank with themselves, they admit that sex is a biological necessity. Therefore, they recognized this and fostered such necessity. Every lad has a girl friend and every lass has a boy friend. They accompany one another most of the time and go out for picnics where they rid themselves of the persistent sexual burden and respond to the call of sex. They return from such picnics so relaxed that they can devote themselves to their studies and work in a way which will bring about an ever increasing measure of prosperity and production. In this manner the whole nation will be going ahead.

But those trivial and superficial minded people who are so enthralled by the Western moral corruption do forget that France could not withstand the first German attacks. It was brought to its knees not only for lack of military training and equipment but also because it was a nation without any desire of national pride, a nation which used to wallow in corruption and was exhausted by sensual pleasures. The French people were afraid that the tall buildings of Paris and its houses of pleasure might be destroyed by bombs. Is this what the so called intellectuals want us to do ?

As for America it is sufficient to quote American statistics which show that 38% of secondary school girls are pregnant. The percentage of pregnency among university undergraduates is less than that because they are more experienced in using contraceptives.

There is no doubt that getting rid of the burden of sex is a worthy goal. Islam pays great attention to this question because it knows very well that the preoccupation with sex will decrease production and confine people to a world of sex from which they cannot depart. But a worthy goal should be realized through worthy means. It cannot be said that polluting society or permitting teenagers to rush out on one another as animals are worthy means.

If some misguided people wrongly believe that the great American production is an outcome of sexual corruption, let them know that it is a purely materialistic production which may result in man's replacement by robots. As for intellectual and spiritual values, it should not be forgotten that America enslaves negroes and subjects them to the worst treatment ever witnessed by humanity. America supports the cause of colonialism in all parts of the world. It is impossible to separate the spiritual decline represented by the submission to animal passions and the spiritual decline manifested in colonialism and slavery — both are related to a kind of decline to which truly civilized nations would not descend.

There is no doubt that the majority of people in these days derive great pleasure from associating with beautiful and elegant women. This is quite true because tasting a number of dishes is more desirable than having to repeat the same dish ! But is pleasure the only goal in life ? And has any one denied that the wild passions have always been highly desirable ? The pleasures of the flesh and the unruly passions are not the discoveries of the western world of the twentieth century. The Greeks, the Romans and the Persians had known such pleasures and were down to their ears in the pleasures of the flesh. But it was the addiction of the said nations to the sensual pleasures that distracted them from their serious pursuits and invariably brought about the end of their rule and supremacy.

Although the West has considerable materialistic potentialities (science, mass production and the mad rush to work) yet its addiction to sensual passions is leading to its partial downfall. But if we do not possess the necessary power because the circumstances of the last two centuries were not in our favour, what benefits do we hope to gain by giving in to our passions in the name of civilisation and progress or for fear of being accused of reactionarism ? If we submit to our unruly passions our circumstances will never improve and we shall always be deteriorating and declining. All those " free thinkers " who advocate the abandonment of the traditions are but colonialist stooges. Colonialism understands and encourages such writers and thinkers and knows how much they serve its evil objectives by corrupting the morals and ethics of people and diverting the interests of the youth to the pursuit of the pleasures and passions.

We often hear many misguided people say : look at women in the western societies — and behold how they have been elevated from mere females to full fledged women. They have become human creatures playing a role in social life. There is no doubt that women after taking regular work and associating with the other sex, have had new experiences which could not have been available if they had confined their activities to looking after their home and children. But let us ask this question : Did such experiences add anything to the capacities of women as such? Or did they add some potentialities while they curtailed others ?

We ask again : Did such experiences add anything to human existence as a whole ? Or did they merely add something while curtailing other aspects ?

The Western woman has become a good friend to man ; she accepts his flirtation and responds to his sexual desires, and she even shares some of his problems but she is no longer a good wife or mother. This is supported by the fact that the rate of divorce in U.S.A. has reached a monstrous degree of 40%. In Europe the rate of divorce is a little lower but keeping mistresses and lovers is a common practice among married people. If the Western woman was a good wife and could settle in a family to which she would devote all her care, the rate of divorce in U.S.A. would not be so high, nor would the escape from home be a common practice in Europe. It should be also pointed out that working women do not have the experiences necessary for good mothers, they would not have the time nor the psychological aptitude to meet their obligations as mothers.

On the other hand, apart from pleasure and delight humanity as a whole has almost gained nothing from the free association of the sexes. There is no doubt that neither the few women who have become deputies, ministers or heads of departments, nor the thousands or millions of them who work in factories, stores, public houses or brothels, could solve the problems of the world. Is it possible that a woman cannot play an effective part in the social life except by making speeches in parliament or signing directives in departments ? No one can say that a woman does not play a prominent part in society when she brings up her children in the proper way and presents the world with good citizens. A woman may be intoxicated by ovation in parliament or admiration in salons and streets but all these are nothing when compared to the danger of supplying the world with motherless generations who have not experienced the love which neutralises the evil desires in their souls. Such love is only given by mothers who are completely devoted to such a sacred duty.

It is true that we should not be too hard on women by depriving them from the pleasures of life, or from asserting their personal existence. But life does not permit us—both men and women—to have our own ways or to assert our existence in the manner we like.

What would happen if we are selfish enough to enjoy ourselves without any limits ? We shall be succeeded by miserable generations whose misery would be the outcome of our selfishness and delinquency. It is not in the interest of women as a sex that future generations may be miserable simply because the women of a particular generation have had excessive pleasures.

Islam cannot be blamed for acting in the interest of all the generations without favouring any one generation to others, because it regards humanity as an endless chain of connected generations. But Islam might be blamed were it to prohibit all kinds of pleasures or fight against natural propensities or repress them.

ISLAM AND SEXUAL REPRESSION

Western psychologists accuse religion of repressing the vital energy of man and rendering his life quite miserable as a result of the sense of guilt which especially obsesses the religious people and makes them imagine that all their actions are sinful and can only be expiated through abstention from enjoying the pleasures of life. Those psychologists add that Europe lived in the darkness of ignorance as long as it adhered to its religion but once it freed itself from the fetters of religion, its emotions were liberated and accordingly it achieved wonders in the field of production.

Such psychologists often say : Do you want us to return to religion ? Do you want to fetter the emotions which, we the progressives, have set free ? Do you want to embitter the lives of the youth by incessantly reminding them of what is right and wrong ?

Let the Europeans say whatever they like about their religion. Whether we believe it or not makes little difference at present because we are not concerned with religion in general : we are discussing Islam.

Before discussing whether or not Islam represses the vital energy we should define the meaning of repression which has been misunderstood and misapplied by both the " cultured " and the half-educated.

Repression is not the result of the abstention from performing the instinctive act. It is the result of believing that the instinctive act is dirty, and of refusing to admit to oneself that such a motive may come to one's mind or engage one's thinking. In this sense repression becomes an unconscious feeling which may not be cured by performing the instinctive act. He who performs the instinctive act but believes that he is committing a degrading and dirty act is a person who suffers from repression, though he may commit such an act twenty times a day. Every time he commits such an act, there shall ensue a conflict within his psyche between what he has done and what he ought to have done. It is this conscious and unconscious conflict which gives birth to complexes and psychological disorders.

This definition of repression is not invented by the writer. It is the definition given by Freud who spent his life in criticizing religion for repressing people's activities. Freud says in his book " Three

Contributions to the Sexual Theory " (p. 82) that " distinction should be made between the unconsciou repression and the abstention from performing the instinctive act — which is a mere suspension of the act ".

Now that we have come to understand that repression is synonymous to the feeling that the instinctive act is dirty rather than a temporary suspension of it, let us proceed with our discussion of repression and Islam.

No religion is as frank as Islam in recognizing the natural motives and treating them as clean and healthy. The Holy Quran says, " *Fair in the eyes of men is the love of things they covet : women and sons : heaped-up hoards of gold and silver, horses branded (for blood and excellence) and (wealth) cattle and well tilled land.*" (*3 : 14*).

In this verse the Quran names the earthly desires and recognizes them as a matter of fact and states that they are desirable things in the eyes of men, but does not object to these desires as such nor does it disapprove of such feelings.

It is true that Islam does not permit people to give way to such desires or to be dominated or enslaved by them. If every one becomes a slave to his passions, life will be running in the wrong direction. Humanity aims at development and improvement ;

it can never achieve such aims as long as it is dominated by its unruly passions which exhaust all the energy and lead it downwards to animalism.

Islam does not allow people to descend to the level of animalism but there is a great difference between this and the unconscious repression which holds that such passions are dirty in themselves and which drives people to abstain from even entertaining such feelings in the name of purification and elevation.

In its treatment of human soul, Islam recognizes in principle, all the natural emotions and does not repress them in our unconscious but it permits the practical performance of such instinctive acts to an extent such as may give a reasonable degree of pleasure without causing any harm or injury to the individual or the community. An individual who is thoroughly absorbed in satisfying his passions brings about an early enervation of his vital energy. Besides, a person who is enslaved by his unruly passions will not be fit for doing anything. All his efforts and thoughts will be devoted to the satisfaction of his desires.

Similarly, the society too suffers a great setback from the exhaustion of the vital energy of its members in one direction alone instead of being used for divers purposes as originally planned by its Creator, as this leads to the neglect of so many other ends that are no less worthy of realisation. It will also lead to the destruction of family ties and to social disintegration : " Thou wouldst think they were united, but their hearts are divided ". This makes it very easy for others to attack and annihilate them like what happened in France.

Subject to the limits that are meant to prevent the individual from inflicting harm upon his ownself, other individuals, the family or society, Islam permits him full enjoyment of the pleasures of life. In fact, Islam frankly calls on people to enjoy the pleasures of life. The Holy Quran says : " *Say, who hath forbidden the beautiful gifts of God which He hath produced for His servants, and the things clean and pure which he hath provided for sustenance ?* " In another verse the Quran says : " *And neglect not thy portion of the world* "; " *Eat of the good things we have provided for you* "; " *Eat and drink but waste not by excess.*"

Islam recognizes the sexual instinct so frankly that the Apostle himself said : " *From the pleasures of the world, perfume and woman were endeared to me ; and the delight of my eye is prayer.*" The sexual instinct is elevated to the rank similar to that of the best perfume on earth, and it is bracketed with prayer which is the best means by which men may come closer to God.

The Apostle once said :

" *A man is recompensed for the sexual act he performs with his wife,*" *and when some of the surprised listeners asked the Apostle of God*: *Is the person rewarded for satisfying his passions ?* *The Prophet answered* ; *Do you not see that if he were to satisfy it in a prohibited manner he would be committing a sin ? So if he satisfies it in a lawful manner he will be recompensed.*" (*Muslim*).

This is why repression will never originate under the rule of Islam. If young people feel the urge of the sexual instinct there is no evil in that, and they need not regard the sexual instinct as a dirty repulsive feeling.

What Islam requires of the young people in this respect, is to control their passions without repressing them, to control them willingly and consciously, that is, to suspend their satisfaction until the suitable time. According to Freud suspension of the performance of the sexual act is not repression. Unlike repression, temporary suspension of the performance of the sexual instinct does not overtax the nerves nor does it lead to complexes and psychological disorders.

This call for controlling the passions is not an arbitrary ordinance intended to deprive people of the pleasures of life, for history bears witness that no nation could safeguard its sovereignty without being able to control its passions or abstain willingly from some permitted pleasures. On the other hand, no nation could withstand international conflicts unless its people were trained to endure hardships and were able to suspend the satisfaction of their desires for hours, days, years as the need of the hour may be.

Hence the wisdom of fasting in Islam . Some libertines, when they talk about fasting say : What is this nonsense which aims at torturing the bodies with hunger and thirst and depriving man of food, drinks and the pleasures which he desires to have ? and for what purpose ? just to comply with arbitrary orders unmotivated by wisdom or reasonable end ?

To such libertines we should say: What is man if he does not exercise his power of restraint ? How can he help humanity if he cannot abstain even for a few hours, from satisfying his desires ? How can we have the patience to fight evil on earth and deprive ourselves as a result thereof of so many pleasures ?

How could the communists — whose propagandists in the Islamic East make fun of fasting and other means of self-restraint, have withstood against the Nazis in Stalingrad if they had not been trained to endure vilest hardships which tortured both their souls as well as their bodies. It is strange that these communists approve of self-restraint when it is ordered by the " State ", the concrete authority that can inflict immediate punishment, but start crying against it when it is demanded by God, the Creator of the state and all living creatures.

It is often said that religion embitters the life of those who follow its rules and lets the ghost of sin haunt them. But this does not apply to Islam which mentions forgiveness far more than it speaks of any castigation.

Sin, according to Islam, is neither a ghoul ever haunting people nor an endless darkness shadowing their lives. Adam's great original sin is not a sword unsheathed in the face of humanity, nor does it require any further purification or ransom : " *Then learnt Adam from his Lord words of inspiration and his Lord forgave him.*"[1] Adam's repentance was accepted simply and without any formalities.

Like their father the children of Adam are not excluded from God's mercy when they commit sin. God knows the limits of their nature and He does not overburden them with what they cannot bear : " *On no soul doth God place a burden greater than it can bear.*" [2] The Apostle says, " *All the children of Adam are wrong-doers, and the best of all wrong-doers are those who repent.*"

The verses of the Quran which describe God's mercy, forgiveness and repentance are very numerous but we are content to quote the following verse :

1. The Holy Quran (2 : 37)
2. The Holy Quran (1 : 286)

" *Be quick in the race for forgiveness from your Lord, and for a garden whose width is that (of the whole) of heavens and of the earth prepared for the righteous — those who spend (freely) whether in prosperity or in adversity ; who restrain anger, and pardon (all) men ; — for God loves those who do good ; and those who having done something to be ashamed of, or wronged their own souls, earnestly bring God to mind, and ask for forgiveness for their sins, — and who can forgive sins except God ? — and are never obstinate in persisting knowingly in (the wrong) what they have done.*"

" *For such the reward is forgiveness from their Lord, and gardens with rivers flowing underneath, — an eternal dwelling : how excellent a recompense for those who work (and strive)* " (3 : 133-136).

How vast and far reaching God's mercy is ! He not only accepts the repentance of souls but also absolves them of their sins and grants them His acceptance and kindness and even elevates them to the ranks of the righteous.

After such mercy could there be the slightest doubt as to God's forgiveness ? How could torture and sin haunt the souls of people when God accepts and welcomes them if they truly utter one word : repentance.

There is no need to quote further texts in support of our argument. But, nonetheless, we shall quote this saying of the Apostle :

" By He in whose hand my soul doth lie, Had you not committed any sin God would have taken you away to replace with others who would commit sin and ask God's forgiveness which will be granted to them."

It is, then, the will of God that He forgives people's sins. In conclusion we quote this wonderful verse of the Holy Quran :

" What can God gain by your punishment, if you are grateful and ye believe ? Nay, it is God that recognizeth (all good) and knoweth all things." (4 : 147).

Yes, what can God gain by torturing people when He loves to grant them His mercy and forgiveness ?

ISLAM AND FREEDOM OF THOUGHT

During the course of a discussion I was told:

" *You are not liberal* ".

" *Why* " ?   I asked him.

" *Do you believe in the existence of a God* ? " he said.

" *Yes, I do.*"

" *Do you pray and fast for Him* ? "

" *I do.*"

" *Well, then you are not liberal.*"

Thereupon I asked him :

" *How do you say that I am not a freethinker* ? "

" *Because you believe in nonsense that has no existence at
    all,*" he told me.

' *And you* ? *what do you people believe in* ? *what
    do you think created the universe and life* ? " I
    asked him.

" *Nature* ! "

" *But what is Nature?* "

" *It is the secret power that is limitless but has got
    manifestations which can be perceived by the
    sense organs,*" he said.

At this I said : " *I understand by this statement of
    yours that you prevent me from believing in an*

unknown power because you want me to believe in another equally unknown power. But the question is that why should I disown my God for the sake of another equally unknown but false god, especially when in the one I find peace, tranquility, and comfort whereas the false God of Nature neither answers my call, nor comforts me? "

This in short is the case of the progressives who talk about freedom of thought. For them freedom of thought is synonymous to the freedom of disowning one's God. This is however not freedom of thought but freedom of atheism. Starting with these premises they accuse Islam of restricting the freedom of thought simply because it prohibits atheism. But the question is : Is freedom of thought and atheism one and the same thing ? and is atheism really a necessary precondition to the freedom of thought ? Misled by the history of European liberalism they overlook the fact that if certain local circumstances necessitated the spread of atheism in Europe, this does not mean that the same thing should happen everywhere in the world.

There is no doubt that the image of Christianity as presented by the church in Europe with its suppression of science, torturing of scientists and passing on a set of lies and superstitions in the name of the word of God drove the free thinkers of Europe to atheism. The intellectuals of Europe had to choose between two irreconcilable attitudes : the natural belief in God or the belief in theoretical and practical scientific facts.

The European intellectuals found in nature a partial escape from the dilemma. So they said to the church, " Take back your God in whose name you enslave us and impose on us burdensome exactions and subject us to tyrannous dictatorship and superstitions. The belief in your God wants us to lead the ascetic life of hermits and recluses, we refuse to do your bidding. We shall therefore have a new God who possesses most of the qualities of the first God but who has no church to enslave us, nor does He impose on us any moral, intellectual or materialistic obligations as your God does."

But in Islam there is no such thing as may drive people to atheism. There are no dilemmas here which puzzle the mind. There is only one God ; He has created all beings and all will return to Him. It is a clear and simple concept which, even the naturalists and atheists may find hard to reject or doubt.

In Islam there are no churchmen such as the European church had. Religion is the common property of all and every Moslem is entitled to benefit from it as much as his natural, spiritual and intellectual equipment may permit. All people are equal and they are treated as they deserve in the light of their deeds in life. The more honoured of all people are the

God-fearing individuals whether they are engineers, teachers, workmen or craftsmen. But religion is not one of these so many occupations. There are no professional churchmen in Islam, so that Islamic worship is observed without the intercession of a churchman. But it is necessary that some people should specialise in the study of jurisprudence and law on which public order is based. The status such specialists in Islamic jurisprudence and constitutional law enjoy is not more than that which their counterparts in other countries do. They are not entitled to any authority or class prestiges over people. They are just the jurisprudents and counsels of the state. It may be pointed out here that Alazhar is a religious institute but it does not have, as the churchmen did, the authority to burn or torture people. All that Alazhar can do is to challenge and criticize an individual's understanding of religion. But on the other hand any one from outside can as well challenge and criticize Alazhar's understanding of religion, for Islam is not the monopoly of any individual or class. Only those persons are considered as an authority on questions of religion who in the light of their deep understanding of it apply it to practical life regardless of their own professions.

When the Islamic rule is established the " ulamas " (Islamic scholars) will not automatically become the governors or ministers or heads of departments.

The only change is that the system of rule will be based on Islamic Sharia (law), the law of God. The engineers will continue to be charged with the engineering works, the doctors will be responsible for medical affairs, the economists will direct economic life of the community with the only change that the Islamic economy alone will then provide them with the guidlines

History bears witness that neither the Islamic faith nor its system of rule ever came into conflict against science or the application of its theories. No scientist in Islam has ever been burnt or tortured for discovering or announcing a scientific fact. True science is not in conflict with the Islamic faith and the belief that God created everything. Islam calls on people to study space and earth and to meditate on their creation in order to discover the existence of God. It should be remembered that many Western scientists who did not believe in God came to discover His existence through the proper scientific research.

There is nothing in Islam which may drive people on to atheism. The advocates of atheism in the East are but blind followers of their erstwhile colonialist masters. They want to be given the freedom to attack the faith and all kinds of worship and to urge people to abandon their religion. But why do they want such freedom ? In Europe people sought to attack religion in order to liberate their minds from superstition and to free people from oppression and tyranny. But if Islamic faith already gives them all the freedom they need to have or they clamour for, why should they attack it ? The truth is that these so-called liberals are not interested in the freedom of thought but are rather more interested in spreading moral corruption and uncontrolled sexual anarchy. They use freedom of thought as a mask to hide their base motives. It is no more than a camouflage in their hideous war against religion and morality. They are against Islam not because it restricts freedom of thought but only because it stands for the liberation of mankind from the dominance of its baser passions.

The advocates of " free thinking " allege that the Islamic system of rule is dictatorial because the state has vast powers. The worst of it, they say, is that the state enjoys immense power and authority in the name of the faith which has a very great attraction for people. So they blindfoldly subject themselves to its tyrannical rule. Thus, they conclude, these vast powers lead to dictatorship and the common people are made slaves with no right to think for themselves. The freedom of thought is lost for ever. None dare challenge the rulers and he who does is accused of rebellion against religion and God.

These false accusations are best refuted by referring to these verses of the Holy Quran : *1. "And*

*their government is by counsel among themselves ". (42 : 38).
2. " And when you judge between people you judge with
justice." (4 : 58).*

Abu Baker, the First Caliph said, " Obey me so
long as I obey God and His prophet. But if I disobey
God or the Prophet I shall no longer be entitled to
your obedience."

Omar, addressed the Muslims saying : " Put
me right if you discover any crookedness in me." One of
the audience retorted : " By God Almighty if we had
found any crookedness in thee we should have put
you right with our swords."

It is true that oppression and tyranny ruled in
the name of religion. It is also true that such oppression
still dominates in some countries in the name of
religion. But is religion the only mask used by dictators ? Did Hitler rule in the name of religion ?
It is now admitted even in Russia, that Stalin was a
tyrant and a dictator who ruled over a police state.
But did Stalin rule in the name of religion ? Do all
tyrants and dictators including Mao Tse Tung, Franco,
Malan in South Africa, Chankai Chek in Nationalist
China, dominate on behalf of religion ? There is no
doubt that the twentieth century which has managed
to get rid of religious domination has witnessed the
most monstrous dictatorships which beguile mankind
by attractive names no less sacred than religion.

No one would defend dictatorship ; no man of free intellect and conscience would approve of it. But any noble principle can be exploited and used as a mask to hide personal ambitions. The French revolution witnessed the most heinous crimes being committed in the name of liberty. But this should not be taken as a pretext for fighting against liberty. Hundreds of innocent people have been imprisoned, tortured or murdered on behalf of the constitution. Should all constitutions be annulled then ? Oppression and tyranny dominated some countries in the name of religion. Should we, therefore, abandon all religions ? It would be right to abandon religion if religion as such were to advocate oppression and injustice. This cannot be said of Islam which established noblest examples of pure justice and equity not only among the Muslims themselves but between Muslims and their fatal enemies as well.

Tyranny is best fought by teaching the people to believe in God and to respect the freedom which is defended and safeguarded by religion. Such people would not allow the ruler to commit injustice, but will keep him within the limits of his legal powers. I do not think that any system has ever aimed at the establishment of justice or the opposition of tyranny as much as Islam did. Islam made it a duty of the people to put the ruler right if he is unjust. The Prophet says " *He who witnesses any vice should change it.*" He also says : *" A word of justice uttered before an unjust ruler is the greatest of jihad (holy war)."*

It was due to these very principles that the people revolted against Othman, the third Caliph, when they believed that he had deviated from the straight course, though the revolution itself brought about even a greater deviation.

In conclusion we would like to drop a word of advice to these " progressive free thinkers " . The true way of liberation is not the abandonment of religion but in giving people the revolutionary spirit which abhors injustice and rectifies the unjust. This spirit is essentially the spirit of the Islamic people.

RELIGION : THE OPIUM OF THE PEOPLE ?

Karl Marx said so . The communist propagandists in the Islamic Orient have not only faithfully repeated this fallacy ever since but they even attempt to apply it to Islam as well.

It might well be said that Karl Marx and other communist pioneers, in view of the peculiar circumstances obtaining in Europe at the time had at least an excuse for revolting against their religion and churchmen. At that time feudalism played a most monstrous role in Europe and particularly in Russia where thousands of people were starved to death every year and millions of people died of consumption and other diseases while cold killed an equal number of people every winter. But the feudal lords still wallowed in the blood of the working people and led a life of licentious luxury enjoying all imaginable kinds of pleasures.

But if the working people ever thought of protesting or even tried to feel the gross injustice to which they were subjected, the clergy would hastily tell them : " Whoever beats you on your right cheek turn the left cheek for him ; whoever takes a part of your garment give him the rest of your clothes."

The churchmen stupefied the people, and tried to divert them from the path of revolution by administering to them dopes of promises of an eternal heaven and paradise where those who bear injustice in this world will live for ever in comfort and pleasure.

If church promises did not work, they would resort to threatening, saying that he who disobeys his feudal lord disobeys God, the Church and the churchmen. It should be remembered that at the time the church itself was the greatest of all feudal lords, with millions of serfs working on its estates. Therefore, it was only natural for the church to join forces with the Tzar and the nobility against the hard working people. They all belonged to the same camp and knew full well that if revolution broke out it would spare no blood-sucker whether he was a nobleman or a churchman.

When both promising and menacing did not work, force was resorted to and punishment was inflicted on the rebels for rebelling against God and religion. That is why religion was regarded as the real enemy of the people there. Hence the remark of Karl Marx : " Religion is the opium of the people."

The communists in the Islamic Orient refer to the behaviour of professional " men of religion " and to how they ingratiate themselves with the rulers at the expense of the hard workers and try to induce them to bear humiliation and injustice by promising them an eternal paradise which will be the recompense of the patient. By such promises " men of religion " try to dope the sensitivity of the hard workers so that the criminal blood-suckers may safely enjoy themselves.

The communists also refer to some of Al Azhar men who used to kiss the hands of kings and interpret the provisions of the glorious Quran to their satisfaction and falsify the spirit and principles of Islam in order to establish the power of the rulers and prevent the hard working people from revolting against them by warning them that they would be committing a rebellion against the word of God which required obedience to the rulers.

All this may have been true; but were such professional men of religion really acting in accordance with the word of God, and the principles of the Islamic faith ? Or did they act in a way that served their personal and selfish interests ?

The fact is that such professional men of religion were acting against the word of God and the principles of Islam. Their case is similar to that of the impious poets, writers and journalists of today who would gladly wallow in dirt if they are sure to obtain thereby some transient though forbidden pleasure. But the crime of such " men of religion " is nonetheless far greater and more monstrous than that of the impious poets, writers and journalists because the men of religion are supposed to guard the word of God, and to know the essence of religion more than any one else. They are supposed to realise the reality of their own attitudes when they falsify the word of God for a worthless price.

Before proceeding further we would, however, like to stress the fact that these are no ' men of re-ligion " as such in Islam and that what they say is not binding on Islam. The misfortune of Islamic people, in fact, sprang up from their ignorance of their own religion.

The false accusation that Islam discourages the rebellion of the working people against oppression is best refuted by the fact that the movement which deposed the ex-king of Egypt was, to start with, essentially a religious movement.

It should also be mentioned that all the liberation movements in the Islamic East were inspired by Islam. The resistance of the Egyptian people against French occupation was led by Muslim (Ulamas) scholars. The rebellion against the injustice of Mohammad Ali was advocated by a religious leader, Omar Makram. The rebellion against the British occupation of the Sudan was led by Almahdi, still another religious leader. The rebellion against the Italians in Libya and the French in Morocco as well as the Kashani revolution against the British occupation, all these were rebellions inspired by and launched in the name of Islam. Every rebellion in the Islamic East contains evidence to show that Islam is a great liberating force directed against all forms of injustice and humiliation.

Communist propagandists often refer to certain verses of the Holy Quran from which they try to extort evidence that Islam calls on people to bear patiently all kinds of injustice and humiliation. They refer to this verse :

" *And do not covet that by which God hath made some of you excel others.*" (*4 : 32*).
and to the following verse :

" *Nor strain thine eyes in longing for the things We have given for enjoyment to parties of them, the splendour of the life of this world, through which We test them : but the provision of thy Lord is better and more enduring.*" (*20* : 131).

Interpreters of the Holy Quran say that the former verse was revealed when a woman asked : Why are men privileged with the obligation of fighting in Allah's way while women are deprived of such a privilege ? According to another and more generally accepted interpretation this verse forbids empty longings that are unaccompanied by practical effort ;

— 297 —

such longings are apt to make man envious, which represents a morbid state of mind and feelings without any material gains such as humanity may benefit from. This verse exhorts the people to do acts which might gain for them merit and honour instead of merely building castles in the air, desiring benefits but not prone to put in any effort for their realisation.

The second verse calls on people to rise higher than merely material considerations and should not covet or think highly of others simply because they happen to enjoy material prosperity. The verse is believed to have been originally addressed to the Apostle (peace and prayer of God be upon him) to belittle the unfaithful who had been endowed with plenty of materialistic pleasures. The Apostle is more elevated than such people because he has right and truth on his side.

Nevertheless, let us suppose, for the sake of sheer argument that these verses advocate contentment with what we have, forbidding to long for what others have. But the question is as to when should such an injunction be put into effect ? When should it be complied with ?

In this connection it may be pointed out that Islam should either be adopted and applied as a whole or wholly abandoned. As a system of life it can bear fruit only if all its demands and its instructions are followed and complied with in toto. This call on the poor and the deprived ever to be patient and refrain from longing for what the rich people have been given is only one side of the picture. On the other hand, there is another call on the rich people to be selfless and spend their money in the way of God. They are threatened with great punishment in the hereafter in case they should in this world stoop to hateful selfishness. If we view the question in this light, the scales of the balance seem to be in perfect equilibrium.

On the one hand, there is the invitation to spend selflessly and on the other, the invitation to purify the spirit from malice and not to humiliate oneself by coveting what others have been given. In this way Islam makes the community live in spiritual peace which is fully in keeping with the economic justice that demands that wealth should be evenly and fairly distributed among the people without making some people to live in luxury or leaving others to suffer privations. When a society adopts the principles of Islam there will be neither injustice nor economic deprivation which the oppressed are called on to accept and bear in non-Islamic communities. But where the rich people do not fulfil their obligations of spending their money in the way of God or to serve the public interest who would call on the poor and the deprived to accept and bear their deprivation ? Surely Islam would not do such a thing. On the contrary, Islam threatens with ill fate in this world as well as in the hereafter all those who submit to injustice or forbear from resisting it. Says the Holy Quran :

" When angels take the souls of those who die in sin against their souls, they say : " In what (plight) were ye ? " They reply : " weak and oppressed were we in the earth." They say : " Was not the earth of God spacious enough for you to move yourselves away (from evil) ? " Such men will find their abode in Hell, — What an evil refuge. Except those who are (really) weak and oppressed — men, women and children — who have no means in their power nor (a guide post) to direct their way. For these there is hope that God will forgive : For God doth blot out (sins) and forgive again and again." (4 : 97-99).

It is an unforgivable crime to submit to injustice on the excuse that one is weak or oppressed on earth. The Quran uses this term, self-oppressors or sinners against their own souls, in describing people who accept a position less than the honourable one which God wants all people to enjoy and calls on them to work with all their might for its achievement.

The call for migration from places where Islam was being persecuted was revealed on a specific occasion, for migration is not the only means of fighting against injustice. There are many other ways for resisting and struggling against injustice. What we want to stress here is that Islam deems it very horrible to bear injustice patiently. Even those who are really very weak and oppressed and have no means in their power nor a guiding post to direct their way have been in the above verse promised only a prayer for forgiveness, and not a certain express forgiveness, though their excuse is clear and their weakness is real. The verse does not mean that God would not forgive such weak and oppressed people — as God would not do injustice to His creatures — but stresses the fact that no one with even an iota of strength should forbear struggling against injustice.

As for the Muslims who are really weak and oppressed, they would not be left to themselves. It is the obligation and the duty of the Islamic nation to fight for their sake and liberate them from oppression :

" And why should ye not fight in the cause of God and of those who, being weak, are ill-treated (and oppressed) — men, women and children whose cry is : " Our Lord! Rescue us from this town, whose people are oppressors." (4 : 75).

God is never satisfied with those who willingly accept and succumb to injustice. They are rather required to struggle against injustice and rescue the oppressed that God may be satisfied with them.

Some people may think that these verses apply to the practice of faith only i.e. when Muslims live among infidels who force them to disown God or prevent them from performing their Islamic duties as Muslims.

Islam does not make any distinction between the performance of religious rites and the improvement of social, economic and political life of the people as they are all based on the basic creed of Islam. It makes no difference whether those who prevent the performance of Islamic rites and the establishment of Islamic system are infidels in name and practice or are Muslims in name but infidels in their practical life. Says the Holy Quran : *" Those who do not rule in accordance with what was revealed by God are the un-believers."* (5 : 44).

Islam prescribes that wealth should not be confined to the few rich people. It also lays down that the state should ensure, by all possible means, security of employment for its subjects : either by providing honourable jobs for them or by supporting them from the Public Treasury in the event of their incapacity to work.

Moreover the Apostle of Islam orders that certain guarantees that have already been described in the foregoing pages should be accorded to Government employees — the guarantees that also apply to those working in private or public establishments. All this forms an integral part of the religion of Islam. It does not as such regard anyone a true Muslim unless he is ready to endeavour to enforce divine law on this earth. The above mentioned verses regarding acceptance of injustice willingly and those who commit injustice towards their own souls apply to those who do not fight for the enforcement of the political, economic and social legislations of Islam.

Let us suppose that people will forbear from struggling against social injustice in compliance with the mistaken understanding of the verses : *" And in no wise covet that by which God hath bestowed His gifts more freely on some of you than on others,"* and the verse : *" And strain not thine eyes towards that which we cause some classes among them to enjoy....... "* What would be the outcome of forbearing to fight against social injustice ?

Wealth will be hoarded up in the hands of a particular class of people sharing it among themselves and depriving the majoirity from it (just as what actually happened under feudalism and capitalism). But this is a monstrous evil ; it violates God's express order that wealth should not be confined to the rich. Another consequence of such a forbearance to fight against social injustice would be that the wealthy people would withhold their wealth or they would spend it on their ownselves and indulge in luxury and extravagant pleasures. The former state is an evil one : " *And there are those who hoard gold and silver and spend it not in the way of God : announce unto them a most grievous penalty.*"(1) In the latter case, there are many verses in the Quran which explicitly prohibit luxury and dub those who live in luxury as impious disbelievers :

" *And we sent not unto any township a warner, but its pampered ones declared : Lo ! we are disbelievers in that which ye bring unto us.*"(2) " *When we decide to destroy a population, we (first) send a definite order to those among them who are given the good things of this life and yet transgress : so that the word is proved true against them : then (it is) that we destroy them utterly.*"(3).

" *And those on the left hand : what of those on the left hand ? In scorching wind and scalding water and in shadow of black smoke, neither cool nor refreshing. Lo ! heretofore they lived in luxury.*"(4)

Nothing but evil will result from people's forbearing from struggling against social injustice. How can Islam be accused of calling on people to accept evil for the pleasure of God. When God Himself says, " *Curses were pronounced on those among the Children of Israel who rejected faith by the tongue of David and of Jesus, the son of Mary : Because they disobeyed and persisted*

---

1. The Holy Quran (9 : 34)
2. Idem   (34 : 33)
3. Idem   (17 : 16)
4. Idem   (56 : 41)

in excesses. Nor did they (usually) forbid one another the iniquities which they committed : evil indeed were the deeds which they did "(1) God treats acceptance of inequity and evil and forbearing them as a mark of disbelief that brings down God's wrath, curses and castigation.

The Apostle says, " *He who sees evil should prevent it* " and he says also that " *The greatest (jehad) struggling for the sake of God is a word of justice said before an unjust ruler.*"

The above mentioned evils can never spread in the society and be acceptable to a ruler unless he is unjust who as such should be resisted and fought against for the sake of God.

No one of sound mind can accuse Islam of enjoining upon people to cringe before injustice or to accept deprivation. Only those who are prejudiced against it or dominated by their lust and passions can dare utter such a falsehood.

The above mentioned verses prohibit the idle longings which are not accompanied with productive effort. They also advocate acceptance of situations such as cannot be altered by any power on earth : the state, society or any people. They are natural, not an artificial outgrowth.

There are many people who have the talents that may bring them fame and popularity. Others

1. The Holy Quran (5 : 81-82)

long to have a similar fame but they do not have the necessary talents to achieve or deserve it. What can the state do in order to satisfy such idle longings ? Can it prevent them from degenerating into morbid malice ? will or can the state " manufacture " a talent for such people ?

Let us take the example of a beautiful woman who captures attention or admiration and a still another one who lacks beauty as well as grace but nonetheless desires to be considered very beautiful so as to attract attention and admiration. What can the state do in order to establish equality in this case ? Or take the case of a married couple living in happiness and love and begetting children who become a source of happiness for them, and another couple that are far from leading a happy life of love with no children to please them despite all medical treatment. How can all the powers on earth try to make up for what the second couple lack in this respect ?

There are innumerable examples of such cases in life. Neither economic solutions nor any scheme of social justice can do anything about it. The only solution in such cases is the acceptance and content-ment with God's provisions that are given out to people in accordance with measures other than the earthly ones, and which recompense this worldly deprivation with the heavenly bliss.

Even from the social and economic points of view, who can say that absolute equality is attainable on this earth ? Is there a single country in the world where all wages and all posts are equal ?

Take for instance life in the Soviet Union, the country that claims to have established absolute equality. Supposing that there is an ambitious workman who longs to become an engineer but his mental ability does not qualify him to become one despite all fair opportunities that are given to him, how can the state help him realize his wish ? Similarly there might be another worker who does not have the physical ability to take up a voluntary workshift for which he can get extra wages, but still he desires to get the extra wages which only the stronger workman can earn. What can the state do in his case ? How can such people enjoy a life of constant worrying, incessant longing and morbid malice ? How can such people properly perform the duties of their work without looking up for the greater power and expecting swollen salaries therefrom. Is it better to cure this malady with fire and sword from without or to remedy it willingly and with one's own initiative from within ?

In short the message of Islam is to work actively for the realisation of lawful desires and to accept willingly that which cannot be altered. But where there is injustice that can be prevented, God would not be pleased with people unless they rebel against and do away with such injustice : " *To him who fighteth in the cause of God — whether he is slain or gets victory — soon shall we give a reward of great (value)."* (4 : 74).

Should there be in the world any religion that can be termed as an opium of the peoples, surely Islam is not that religion, as it disowns all forms of injustice and threatens those who accept it with most grievous chastisement.

ISLAM AND NON-MUSLIM COMMUNITIES

It has always been said that the attitude of non-Muslim communities towards Islamic rule is a critical and delicate question which many people hesitate to discuss for fear of causing dissension between Muslims and non-Muslims.

Let us be frank with the Christians of the Islamic East and put to them these questions :

What do they fear from the rule of Islam ? Are they afraid of the Holy texts of Islam or of the manner of their application ?

As for the provisions, we may quote the Holy Quran : " *God forbids you not, with regard to those who fight you not for (your) Faith nor drive you out of your homes, from dealing kindly and justly with them: For God loveth those who are just* " (1)
and

" *The food of the people of the Book is lawful unto you and yours is lawful unto them. (Lawful unto you in marriage) are (not only) chaste women who are believers, but chaste women among the people of the Book.* " (2)

---

1. The Holy Quran (**60 : 8**)
2. Idem   (6 : 6)

We should also refer to the general principle in Islamic jurisprudence : " They shall have the same obligations and rights as we."

The Islamic Holy texts enjoin Muslims to treat non-Muslims in a kind and fair manner. Apart from the rights and obligations involving worship, they are equal to Muslims with respect to all other rights and obligations related to social life and the rights of citizens. In addition, Islamic faith strives to strengthen the links connecting the non-Muslims with Muslims by encouraging Muslims to visit them and to eat their food, which is the custom of close friends.

Moreover, Islam tries to make the relationship grow closer by permitting inter-marriage , the strongest social bond, between Muslims and non-Muslims.

As to the practical application of the Islamic Holy texts we had better quote a European Christian, who cannot be accused of bias or prejudice, Sir T. W. Arnold in his book " The Preaching of Islam ": " That force was not the determining factor in these conversions may be judged from the amicable relations that existed between the Christian and the Muslim Arabs. Muhammad himself had entered into treaty with several Christian tribes, promising them his protection and guaranteeing them the free exercise of their religion and to their clergy undisturbed enjoyment of their old rights and authority." [1]

He goes on to say that :

" From the examples given above of the toleration extended towards the Christian Arabs by the victorious Muslims of the first century of the Hijrah and continued by succeeding generations, we may surely infer that those Christian tribes that did embrace Islam, did so of their own choice and free will." [2]

" When the Muslim army reached the valley of Jordan and Abu Ubaydah pitched his camp at Fihl, the Christian inhabitants of the country wrote to the Arabs, saying. " O Muslims, we prefer you to the Byzantines, though they are of our own faith, because you keep better faith with us and are more merciful to us and refrain from doing us injustice and your rule over us is better than theirs, for they have robbed us of our goods and our homes ". [3]

He also tells us that :

" Such was the state of feeling in Syria during the campaign of 633-639 in which the Arabs gradually drove the Roman army out of the province. And

---

1. The Preaching of Islam. P.P. 47-48.
2. Ibid P. 51.
3. Ibid p. 55.

when Damascus, in 637, set the example of making terms with the Arabs, and thus secured immunity from plunder and other favourable conditions, the rest of the cities of Syria were not slow to follow. Emessa, Arethusa, Hieropolis and other towns entered into treaties whereby they became tributary to the Arabs. Even the patriarch of Jerusalem, surrendered the city on similar terms. The fear of religious compulsion on the part of the heretical emperor made the promise of Muslim toleration appear more attractive than the connection with the Roman Empire and a Christian government, and after the first terrors caused by the passage of an invading army, there succeeded a profound revulsion of feeling in favour of the Arab Conquerors." (1).

This is the evidence given by a Christian scholar on Islam. What is it then that the Christians fear from Islamic rule ?

It may be that the Christians are afraid of Muslim fanaticism. If this is true, it seems that they have no idea of what fanaticism is. Here are a few examples of fanaticism.

Courts of inquisition set up by the Christian Church were primarily meant to exterminate the Muslims of Spain. The said courts tortured Muslims,

---

(1) P· 55 : The Preaching of Islam.

in a monstrous way which has never been experienced before. People were burnt alive, their finger nails were pulled off, their eyes were put out, and their limbs were amputated. This torture was inflicted in order to force people to change their religion and adopt a particular Christian creed.

Have the Christians of Islamic East ever suffered such treatment ?

Massacres are carried out for the extermination of Muslims in Europe: Yugoslavia, Albania, Russia or countries under European rule such as : North Africa, Somalia, Kenya, Zanzibar or in other countries : India and Malaya. Such massacres are staged sometimes on the pretext of the purgation of ranks and sometimes for the maintenance of peace and security.

Another significant example is the treatment of Muslims in Ethiopia which has ancient historical, geographical, cultural and religious links with Egypt. It has a mixed population of Muslims and Christians. Although Muslims account for 35%—65% of the total population there is not a single school where Islamic faith or Arabic is taught. Private schools which the Muslims open at their own expense are subjected to exorbitant taxes and inconveniences which lead to their closing and disheartening those who may think of opening new schools. In this way

Islamic teaching is confined to primitive ways of teaching.

Until very recently — just before the Italian invasion — a Muslim who could not pay a debt to his Christian creditor was taken in slavery by the Ethiopian Christian. The Muslim was caught, sold and tortured under the government's sight.

It goes without saying that there is not a single Muslim in the cabinet or in any key post to represent the one third of the population.

Has the Christians of the Islamic world ever experienced such a treatment ? Would they accept reciprocal treatment ?

That is the real fanaticism.

The Communists believe that the real existence of man is essentially an economic existence. If so, have the Christians living in Islamic countries ever been denied the right to acquire and dispose of property or to amass wealth ? Have they ever been denied on account of their religious belief, the right to have education, to join public service or promotion to higher public posts ?

As for the moral and spiritual existence, it should be stressed that the Christians living under Islamic rule have never been subjected to any form of religious persecution with the exception of the very rare incidents engendered by the British Colonialists for the purpose of sowing dissension and diversion. It is alleged that the imposition of tribute on non-Muslims is the result of religious discrimination. The best refutation of this baseless accusation lies in the words of T. W. Arnold, who says :—

" On the other hand, when the Egyptian peasants, although Muslim in faith, were made exempt from military service, a tax was imposed upon them as on the Christians in lieu thereof."[1]

" As stated above, the jizyah was levied on the able bodied males, in lieu of the military service they would have been called upon to perform had they been Muslimans ; and it is very noticeable that when any Christian people served in the Muslim army, they were exempted from the payment of this tax. Such was the case with the tribe of al-Jurajimah, a Christian tribe in the neighbourhood of Antioch, who made peace with the Muslims, promising them to be their allies and fight on their side in battle, on condition that they should not be called upon to pay jizyah and should receive their proper share of the booty."[2]

---

1. The Preaching of Islam P. 63.

2. Idem   P. 62.

From this it is clear that the imposition of tribute is not the result of any religious discrimination. The truth is that the tribute was imposed on all those who did not take part in military service regardless of their religious belief. It would be useful to refer in this respect to the following Holy verse :

" Fight those who believe not in God nor the Last Day, nor hold that forbidden which hath been forbidden by God and His Apostle, nor acknowledge the Religion of Truth (even if they are) of the People of the Book, until they pay the Jizya with willing submission and feel themselves subdued." (9 : 29).

It should be pointed out that this verse refers to non-Muslims who wage war against Islam. It does not apply to the non-Muslims living in Islamic countries.

In conclusion I should like to warn that the seeds of dissension between Muslims and non-Muslims living in Islamic countries are shown by colonialists as well as by communists. The communist devils address each community in accordance with its particular aspirations. They address the working classes saying " If you adopt communism we shall hand over all factories to you. While speaking to peasants, they promise to give them the lands.

On talking to unemployed graduates they say, "If you become communists you will get the jobs that fit in with your qualifications."

As for the youth suffering from sexual repression, the communists promise them a free society, where every one can act as one likes without intervention by law or subjection to traditions.

The communists address Christians in the following manner : " If you adopt communism we shall destroy Islam, the religion that discriminates among people on account of their religion." *But " it is a grievous thing that comes from their mouths as a saying, for, what they say is nothing but falsehood."* [1]

It cannot be said that Islam distinguishes among people on account of their religion because Islam confers the essential rights on all people without any distinction. Islam brings all people together on a purely human basis and at the sametime guarantees them absolute freedom to adopt the religion of their choice, under its own care and protection.

Besides, as the Christians of the East are also anxious to retain their historical links with Muslims and protect their mutual interests, let us hope that they would not listen to these propagandists or dissenters.

_____

1. The Holy Quran (18 : 5)

ISLAM AND IDEALISM(1)

We are often asked : "where is the Islam you Muslims talk about ? When was it ever applied to life in its true form ? You are never tired of saying that it is an excellent ideal system but did it ever exist in actual life ? If asked about its practical form you cannot but refer to a short period stretching over the life of the (Holy) Prophet and the early caliphate or rather the first two caliphs. You are

---

(1) " Idealism " is a word very popular in the East where it is used to describe a system that embraces in itself all that is best. From this it must be clear that we are not using this term in this sense with regard to Islam as we are in this book concerned with the aspersions cast against it. We use this word rather in the sense in which it is generally used in the West. According to the western interpretation idealism means soaring high in the realm of ideas leaving the people below on earth to their fate, deprivations, hunger, misery and inequity. Practically nothing is done in order to do away with these evils. The people are left to themselves to groan under them. This is why the Europeans came to hate the word " idealism ", quite justifiably of course, as it called on people to accept the hell of feudalism, to suffer tribulations and disgrace, while it talked on to them about philosophical subjects such as had no meaning or use for them in their every day life. Dry and empty as these abstract discussions were, they were also devoid of all sense. Naturally human reason could not but abhor this sophistry. It is because of this historical background that the Europeans ridicule and hate all forms of idealism. Anxious to exploit this situation the communists betray their own ignorance when they accuse Islam of a similar, barren and visionary idealism.

never tired of saying about Omar-bin-al-Khatab in particular, that he was the embodiment of what Islam stood for ; you depict him in most resplendent colours but when we inquire about the conditions of life prevailing during his reign we find nothing but " layers of darkness one above another " — feudalism, inequity, tyranny, reactionarism and backwardness. You assert that Islam gives the nation the right to chastise its rulers in case they fail to carry out their obligations but when except in the early caliphate the people were ever allowed to choose their own rulers, let alone chastising them ? You also say that Islam offers a very just economy with a fair distribution of wealth but when even in the early caliphate were the differences among the people levelled ? You tell us that it makes the providing of employment for all of its citizens incumbent upon the state, but what about those millions of unemployed who sometimes lived on begging or were otherwise doomed to a life-long privation and poverty ? You also speak about the rights of women in Islam but did she ever in fact enjoy these rights ? Isn't it a fact that she has never been able to exercise them because of the unfavourable socio-economic conditions ? You talk about the spiritual elevation of men as a result of their fear of God and establishment of the relations as a consequence thereof between the rulers and the ruled, between different classes of the community on the basis of a mutual co-operation for the sake of justice and virtue but when save in a comparatively rare period was this spiritual elevation ever witnessed ? Did it ever provide a check on the rulers to prevent them from usurping the right of the poor subjecting them to injustice and cruelty ? Did it prevent them from trampling underfoot the liberties of the people and from exposing them to disgrace and humiliation ? In fact you are talking about a dream land which does not exist in the world of reality, and the short period of which you are so fond of proves nothing beyond the fact that there were certain extraordinary persons who did perform mighty deeds such as others can never hope to do. It is an exception for it was never afterwards repeated, nor is it likely to be witnessed again."

This is what the communists and their likes assert. Many of the Muslims too are unfortunately found to be the prey to this sort of propaganda as they know nothing about the Islamic history save that taught to them by their imperialist masters.

Before proceeding further we would like to stress a basic difference between a pure idealism with no instance to show that it is practicable or applicable to conditions of life, and an idealism such as is fully attainable with historical evidence to support its claim that it can not only be successfully applied to practical life but is also fully capable of directing its course. As such the question that props up is : is

Islam by its very nature merely a utopian ideal that exists nowhere, nor is capable of being practised in this world, its whole texture being fabricated out of purely imaginary and fictitious elements ? or is it a practical system of life but may not necessarily be applied to life with equal success or in a similar manner during all the periods of human history ? Evidently there is a very great difference between these two forms of idealism. If Islam be an ideology of a purely abstract character, then there is no longer any hope whatever of its being ever applicable to the actual conditions of living howsoever great a change the social circumstances and conditions of life might undergo in future. But if it is a practical system of life and only the external conditions of life intervene in the way of its fullest application, then the case is quite different. In such a case there is every hope that it might be materialised in life if and when these unfavourable conditions of life change or become favourable to it. Which of the two cases is applicable to Islam, the former or the latter ?

The answer is not far to seek as the matter is so clear that there can hardly be two opinions about it. That Islam has once been already fully applied in human history proves beyond any doubt as to its being a practical system of life that is fully capable of being practised or adopted by man. It also proves that its basis is not an imaginary or a fictituous one.

Men are what they were or have been before, there being no change in the human nature as such. Therefore what happened once might happen again and again. Modern progressionists say that it cannot rehappen and therefore Islamic revival is a hopeless task but may we ask them if they want to say that man in the early days of Islam had attained to such a high pinnacle of moral perfection, as humanity is unable to regain those heights ever again. How do they justify this stand of theirs in the face of their own claim that humanity is constantly advancing forward and ever marching ahead ?

The question as to why the like of the early caliphate is not seen in the subsequent history save once in the beginning and later on during the extremely short periods sparsed here and there in Muslim history such as the reign of Umar-bin-Abdul Aziz for example, calls for a close study of the problem. Its answer, however, is clearly imprinted on the pages of history, either in the form of a local phenomenon witnessed in the Islamic world or as a universal truth exhibited in the life history of mankind.

We needs must in this respect refer to the following two facts : *firstly*, the great leap that humanity strode forward with the help of Islam and the deep abyss from the bottom of which Islam lifted it to the lofty heights of moral refinement witnessed in the early caliphate was a phenomenon such as cannot be ex-

plained in terms of ordinary physical laws of life ;
it was rather a miracle out of the so many other
miracles brought about by Islam on the face of this
earth. But it was made possible only after years of
preparation and a thorough moral reorientation of
those great heroes of Islam who exemplified and
embodied this great miracle in their persons as well
as in their whole conduct in life.

But Islam spread with such a lightning speed
in the world that there is hardly any parallel to it
in the history of the different historical movements
either in the earlier or in the subsequent periods.
This is just another miracle brought about by Islam
that is hard to explain through any materialistic or
economic interpretation of history such as with which
the communists and the materialists are wont to
explain away human history. This speedy propagation
of Islam, however, brought into its folds very many
nations who were far from being fully acquainted
with the real spirit of Islam, nor did they understand
the real significance of its socio-economic and political
system. Unfortunately it was not possible for the
Muslim governments of the time to arrange for the
doctrinal instruction or moral education of these
converts such as was given to early Muslims of Arabia.
Consequently, the Islamic empire expanded and the
number of the believers also multiplied but Islamic
principles and teachings never found way into the

hearts of these large hosts of converts. The rulers no longer feared the public opinion while trampling underfoot the commandments of Islam. They usurped the people's liberties and subjected them to all forms of injustice as is known by the history of the Ommeyeds, Abassides, Turks and Mamlukes. In the absence of a well-formed and educated public opinion they could easily treat Islam as a plaything and usurp the rights of the people.

Secondly, the great advancement that Islam effected in human life cannot be termed as a physical or a natural phenomenon for in one great leap it raised humanity from the lowest depths of slavery and serfdom to the highest and most ideal state of social justice yet experienced by mankind under any other social system it has so far tried. Islam freed it from the dominance of unruly passions and elevated it to the highest realms of moral perfection ever witnessed in the whole range of human history.

It was Islam that made men win these surprisingly lofty moral heights during its early period as the spiritual force exemplified in the personality of the Holy Prophet and his Companions was an extraordinary one. It was this force that raised men to a plane far higher than they could ordinarily attain and made them perform mighty works very much akin to miracles. When, however, this mighty impulse ebbed away the people reverted to their former state from their erstwhile sublime state of moral and spiritual existence, although they still retained a spark at least of the divine light. It is the pages of history illumined by this divine light which we intend to point out to our fellowmen in this treatise. But this does not mean as some people have wrongly assumed that it requires the constant presence of the Prophet himself and his companions to bring about even the smallest change in practical life such as was effected by Islam, for that which was a miracle in the world of politico-economic relationships thirteen hundred years ago, has now, thanks to the experiences gained by mankind or by the Muslim community itself over the centuries, become a task for the performance of which man is fully equipped. Therefore if we should want to apply Islam to the modern conditions of life making due allowance for the high moral excellence exemplified in the lives of the early Muslims we would not have to move forward at the miraculously high speed such as characterised the early history of Islam, for the various experiences and the progress since made by man has already brought us much closer to the lofty pinnacle of the Islamic ideal. Its achievement has, as a consequence thereof become much easier, the effort required also being far less arduous. A few examples from the modern life may suffice to illustrate the truth of what we have said above.

Most of the nations in the modern times elect their rulers through general elections, and also have the right to suspend or dismiss them if they should fail in discharging their obligations towards the people. But this is no more than a modern application of an important feature of the Islamic system of government that was instituted by Islam more than thirteen hundred years ago. Surely this was a miracle in the age of the caliphs Abu-Bakr and Omar, but not in this modern world of ours ; its realisation is now completely within our means provided we should honestly wish to enforce it in our lives. For if we can take it from England or America, why cannot we as well adopt it in the name of Islam, especially when it is already there in Islam ?

Then there is the question of guaranteeing the basic needs of its employees by the state. About this too there is the explicit commandment of the Prophet (peace be on him) that all employees of the state shall be provided with their basic needs. It was this very commandment that communism carried into effect in the twentieth century notwithstanding the fact that Islam had already done so without resorting to a dictatorship of the proletariate such as communism could not do without. If we are inclined today to guarantee these basic needs to the state-employees, why should we not follow the lead of Islam rather than imitate communism ?

Thus the problem we are dealing with in the final analysis crystalises to the fundamental question : Is a particular socio-economic and political system practicable or not ? This is the only criterion whereby the practicability or otherwise of a system can be judged aright. Judging from this stand-point we find that the Islamic system of life is in fact a practical system of life, for it was the first system ever practically applied to human life on the face of this earth.

There is no truth in what the communists and their camp-followers say that the modern life is raised on a scientific foundation while Islam is a system based on passions and pious intentions. That this is absolutely false may be realised by the fact that the Islamic law, for instance, does not at all rest on feelings or emotions of men. Similarly early caliphs did not rest their decisions on wishful thinking or the intentions of men when conferring with their councils or seeking some legal interpretation and application of Islamic law.

The fact is that Islam does not rely on law alone. It no doubt frames various laws but it first of all wants to civilize human beings from within so that they would willingly submit to the law if and when it is enforced not only because of any outside fear of the government but because of their own moral initiative from within. Undoubtedly this is the most excellent achievement so far gained by mankind in the world of politics. But still the law is there all the time although it is invoked only when the general good calls for it. In such cases it is enforced without any regard whatsoever of the feelings of people to such an extent that caliph Othman said : " God restrains with authority that which is not retrained by the Quran."

Some writers while arguing that the revival of Islam is impossible allege that men like Omar are not born every day ; personalities like his are exceptions and not met with frequently in history. But such a line of reasoning betrays their own barrenness of thought. For, it is not the person of Omar— the typical man produced by Islam — that we stand in need of for the enforcement of the Islamic law but rather the laws framed or legal precedents left behind by him. Thus for instance Omar ordered that the hands of a thief shall not be cut in case there is a possibility of his being driven to it due to some external economic or social exigency. Surely this legal precedent does not necessarily call for the presence of a man like Omar to apply it to practical life, as it was nothing but an interpretation of the basic principle of the Islamic jurisprudence which lays down that in cases of doubtful nature the legal punishment should be avoided. There is no external or internal check upon us such as due to which we may not be able to enforce it in our practical life just because there is no Omar amongst us.

Similarly Omar laid it down that the ruler was fully authorised to take of the excess of the rich people's wealth and distribute it among the poor as is nowadays being done for instance in England. It did not need a Omar to enforce this law in England which is sufficient to prove its practicability in the modern world. This ruling of his was also based on the well-known Quranic principle concerning riches : " *in order that it may not (merely) make a circuit between the wealthy among you.*" (59:7). Omar also enunciated the right of the state to institute an inquiry about the wealth amassed by the governors with a view to know as to whence they had acquired it ; if it was their own or misappropriated from public funds or gained through unlawful means. This has also become almost a universal practice in the contemporary world, although there is of course no Omar here among us. He also made it a law that a foundling shall be looked after by the state and his expenses defrayed from the public exchequer for he could not be held responsible or left to suffer for the sin committed by the parents. Europe and America at last recognised this framing laws to that effect in the twentieth century, which again shows that so far as the enforcement or the application of the law is concerned the presence of a Omar is not inevitable. We need Omar not just because he was a man of towering personality but because he is the most outstanding legist of the early period of Islam besides his being so deeply imbued with the spirit and understanding of Islam. As for his personal life we may follow it with benefit for it helps us to ascend to higher planes of being and affords the Muslims of all times to come with a sublime and noble example to follow. But even if we fail in following his personal example, our observance of the laws enacted by him might suffice in practical life, for these would enable us to stand on our legs and not merely imitate or follow blindfoldly the laws and constitutions imported from foreign lands.

There is also still another great misunderstanding prevalent against Islam. It is said that Islam was never fully established on this earth save in the early caliphate period. It is correct that Islam was never enforced in its true form except during the short period of Omar bin Abdul Aziz after the early caliphate; yet it does not at all mean that Islam as a religion and a system of life had ceased to exist after the caliphate period. In the subsequent years it was the government only that had suffered a morbid change from the point of view of Islam partly or totally. The rest of the society remained as Islamic in spirit as ever.

It did never recognize the division of the people into the "haves," and ' have-nots ' or into masters and slaves. Rather they were all united in a universal brotherhood sharing with one another the labour as well as the fruits thereof.

The law of the land of Islam always ruled supreme in all the different parts of the Islamic world. The people were never left to the mercy of feudal lords as happened in Europe. The Islamic traditions lived and may be witnessed in the history of wars of Islam against its enemies. A perusal of the crusades particularly during the days of Salah-ud-Din Al Ayubi, may suffice to convince one of the veracity of the above statement. The conduct of the Muslims in carrying out their international agreements even during their latter history was no less sublime and glorious. Their love for knowledge and regard for civilization made the Islamic world a favourite haunt of all true seekers of knowledge and arts. It was this torch of knowledge lighted by Islam that finally set ablaze the whole of Europe and made it march ahead on the path of progress and development.

In short Islam is not an ideal system in the derogatory sense this term is commonly understood to imply in the West. It is rather a perfectly practical system of life that has already been once tried by humanity. Mankind as such can adopt it now with as much success as it did thirteen hundred years ago thanks to the experience gained since, for it has brought mankind much closer and nearer to it; realisation. On the other hand, it is communism which may rightly be dubbed as a mere idle idealism with no successful practical application of it so far to human life. The stage of real communism, we are told, has not yet been attained : the world is rather steadily moving towards that ideal stage. When all the world shall be brought under the control of a single world communist state and all wealth distributed evenly among all its citizens, then will the real stage of communism be attained. Then the class-war between the ' haves ' and the ' have-nots ' shall be done away with once for all as it is the uneven distribution of wealth that is the sole cause of this class warfare.

This communist dreamland is a utopia such as would never be materialized in this world of reality. It belongs under the realm of delusion. Its basic assumptions, that the human beings can ever be artificially made equal in possessing similar means of production and that all class-war shall come to an end when and if wealth is distributed evenly among all people and that humanity cannot progress except through interclass warfare, are altogether baseless and untrue. It represents an idealism such as can fascinate the fools only. It originated out of materialism and ironically enough is supposed to be based on scientific principles and facts of life.

ISLAM AND COMMUNISM

"As we have already submitted, Islam stands for all that is good, healthy and desirable in life. It is the religion for all times, generations and societies but as the Islamic world during the last four centuries has been in a state of constant depression, the portion of the Islamic law dealing with economic problems remained static. Why shouldn't we then adopt Islam as a creed to edify our souls and purify thoughts and embrace communism as the economic system to solve our economic problems as it would in no wise effect our social set up or any aspect thereof. We shall thus be able not only to safeguard our morals, social traditions and customs but also have at the same time one of the most modern economic systems of the present times to resolve our economic problems."

The reasoning such as this given above is a part of the diabolical game the communists are out to play now since a long time. To begin with they adopted an aggressive attitude towards Islam in the East and cast various doubts about it. But when they found that this had rather increased Muslims' attachment to Islam, they changed their strategy and resorted to fraud and deception. Thus they reasoned that :

" Communism does not at all interfere with Islam, as it is basically just another name for social justice and stands for the responsibility of the state towards its citizens to provide them with the basic needs of life. Do you mean to say that Islam is opposed to social justice by alleging that it is opposed to communism. Surely Islam cannot oppose such a system based on social justice."

This diabolical reasoning is similar to that resorted to by the imperialists before this. They too had started with attacking Islam openly but when they found that it had only put the Muslims on their guard and they were watchful, they resorted to another course. They said : " The West is interested only in the spread of civilization in the East ; how can Islam be against civilization when it is itself the father of civilization ? " They assured the Muslims that they could adopt this western civilization without giving up their fastings, prayers, and mystic practices, although they were sure that if the Muslims once succumbed to their civilization they would no longer be able to retain their Islamic character with the result that within a few generations this civilization would overpower them once for all. They proved right. Consequently there arose a generation among the Muslims after sometime who was completely ignorant about Islam, who rather felt a repulsion from it without any knowledge, or reason whatsoever.

It is this very game of fraud and deception that the communists are playing today. They say that the Muslims can at once remain Muslims, can pray, fast and perform esoteric rituals and adopt communism as an economic system, for it does not at all meddle with their religion. Why should they then hesitate in embracing it ? But while thus arguing they know very well that Muslims will no longer remain Muslims if they once but succumbed to its temptation. In such a case they are sure to remould them in a few years' time after their own philosophy of life and put an end to Islam and all it stands for, because the age we are living in is one of rapid movement and dynamism which means that great changes can very easily be brought about in a comparatively very short period of time. But inspite of all these facts there are very many Muslims who willingly allow themselves to be hoodwinked by such a spurious reasoning as it provides them with an excuse at least to avoid hard struggle in carrying out their unpleasant duties as Muslims promising them at the same time freedom from cumbrous task of finding their own way, use their own reason and exert themselves in constructive activities. They would rather just like to sit down and dream idle dreams and let themselves be guided by others.

We would at this point like to stress the fact that in principle Islam does not oppose any system such as is basically not antagonistic to its principles and serves the Muslim community in solving its problems arising out of the changed conditions of life. The fact, however, is that communism does not at all see eye to eye with Islamic ideology, although it might in some respects superficially resemble Islam. The Muslim community which already possesses the best system, cannot pass by Islam and instead adopt communism, capitalism or materialistic socialism though they might in certain respects appear to be similar to it, for God has expressly commanded that : *" And they who do not judge in accordance with that which is revealed by God, they are indeed the unbelievers."*(1).

Can we in reality embrace communism and yet live on as Muslims ? The answer is a big No, for, when we apply communism (erroneously or dishonestly described as being a purely economic system) we find that it is opposed to Islam in theory as well as in practice. Their collision is inevitable, for the simple reason that it cannot be helped or avoided.

That theoretically both stand opposed to each other in so many respects may well be judged from the following points :

Firstly, communism rests on a purely materialistic basis : it does not recognize anything save that perceived by sense organs : what is not perceivable

---

1. The Holy Quran (5 : 47)

by these sensory organs is unreal,, nonsense and has no existence whatsoever or if it does exist it is so insignificant that one need not at all bother about it. Engels said : "Matter is the only real thing in the world." And the materialists argue that : "Human reason is just a manifestation of matter which reflects the external material environment surrounding it." They go on to say that what is called soul does not at all have an independent existence of its own but is rather a product of matter. Thus we see that communism is a purely materialistic ideology which ridicules all forms of spiritualism dubbing them all as unscientific. Islamic ideology, on the other hand declines to concede to such a narrowing down of human sphere of activities or degrade man to such low levels of existence. It looks upon man rather as a being that aspires to soar high in the realms of spirit and thought, although he walks on earth and possesses a physical body. Nor are his needs limited to food, shelter and sexual gratification as Karl Marx claimed. A question might at this stage be raised in the minds of some readers : How can this materialistic philosophy affect us when we shall have nothing to do with it : we shall adopt only the economic programme of communism and retain all our basic creeds, our God, our Apostle, and our spiritual system. They cannot be affected by the economic programme we might adopt as it is something quite different from the things described above and has an independent existence of its own. Let none be under this illusion, for as the communists hold, there exists a strong affinity between the economic system and the basic creed, ideology and outlook upon life of a people ; they cannot be viewed in isolation : they are closely inter-related, for they are based on the same economic system which is raised on a purely materialist philosophy of life as has been clarified by the communist pioneers Engels and Marx in their writings.

The communists, for instance, also believe in dialectical materialism. They hold that it is the conflict of the opposites (the ' haves ' and the ' have nots ' or workers and capitalists) that is the only real though insidious factor behind all economic and human progress that mankind has achieved so far starting from the first communist age and moving on to slavery, then feudalism, capitalism and then the final communist age. It is with this very dialectical materialism that they justify their stand-point and prove the final emergence of communism as the victor out of the present ideological warfare. They claim that there is a close scientific relationship between communism and this theory of dialectical materialism, in which there is no place whatsoever for any concept of God, His apostles or their message, for in their arrogance they think that all these things are but merely an outcome of the interplay of economic forces; they have no meaning or signficance apart from the economic circumstances that engendered them. As such they lose all their importance in human life and are simply worthless in interpreting or defining life or determining its true objectives. The one and the only factor of importance is the means of production which if changed, affects the whole human existence and revolutionises it. The fallacy and weakness of communist's view of human history is amply proved by the fact that it fails to offer any adequate explanation of the great revolution brought about by Islam in Arabia, for it cannot point out any change in the means of economic production in Arabian peninsula or even in the whole of the contemporary Islamic world that might be referred to as having caused the emergence of the Holy Prophet in that part of the world bringing with him a completely new system of life.

This is quite sufficient to show that Islam and communism stand diametrically opposed to each other. How can the two be said to be at one then ? The Muslims who believe in the Beneficence of God as well as His immense Grace embracing all His creatures and who believe that it is God who sends to them His apostles to guide them aright and who believe that Islam is not subject to the economic exigencies but ascends far above them, how can such Muslims adopt with impunity the communism which holds that all the different stages of human progress are determined by the interplay of the opposing forces alone, thus leaving no place for God's will or any other factor or initiative save that lent to it by economic existence, the pressure of need.

Secondly, man as viewed by communism is just a passive being whose will has no importance whatever in the face of the material and economic forces. Karl Marx said : " The mode of production of the material means of existence conditions the whole process of social, political and intellectual life. It is not the consciousness of men that determines their existence, but, on the contrary, it is their social existence that determines their consciousness."

In Islam, on the other hand, we find that man is viewed as an active being with a free will of his own that is subject to the higher will of God alone. Says the Holy Quran: "*And He has subjected to you, as from Him, all that is in the heavens and on earth.*" (1) Thus Islam makes it clear that it is man who enjoys supreme power and position in this earth with all the material and economic forces being there to do his bidding. Islam itself is a case in point in this respect. Its progress was not limited or directed by any process of dialectical materialism. The early Muslims never even for a single moment felt that the economic existence of man alone played a decisive role in shaping his destiny or that it was something beyond his conscious control as Marx said. They on the contrary did consciously shape their economy in accordance

1. The Holy Quran (45 : 13)

with the guidance of God and His apostle basing all their social relationships on the teachings of Islam : they freed slaves without any consideration of economic gains or initiative inducing them to it ; and they did in fact never witness the establishment of feudalism in their lands although it had been the most prevalent system for centuries in Europe and in the world at large.

The adoption of the communist economy must inevitably lead to the adoption of the communist philosophy, the philosophy which makes man a mere plaything of the economic forces that take their way quite independent of men's will for they can neither change their course, nor can they effect their working in any way as it is simply impossible and therefore unthinkable.

Thirdly, as we have already pointed out in the chapter on "Private Ownership," it is next to impossible to divorce an economic system from the social philosophy behind it. Therefore if we accept communism as an economic programme we must also inevitably embrace along with that the social philosophy it offers and which states that society is the only real thing, the individual having no importance whatever save as a member of a community. This is a position quite contrary to that taken up by Islam, for it attaches great importance to the individual and relies more upon him than on society for the realization of its ends. Islam civilizes man from within so that he would willingly discharge all his responsibilities as a member of a community. Thus it elevates man to the position of a conscious member of society with a will of his own, choosing his own job as well as the place he would like to work in freely. He enjoys freedom to comply with the orders of the ruler or refuse to obey him if the ruler should happen to transgress the bounds set by God's obedience and Islam. Thus Islam makes every individual a guardian of the community's morals besides holding him responsible for the eradication of all forms of evils. But such a thing cannot for obvious psychological and practical reasons happen in a society wherein the individual is reduced to the status of an insignificant midget or a worthless manikin, whose destiny is solely shaped and controlled by the government as it alone controls all economic means of production.

Last, we must also remember that the communist philosophy is based on the assumption that it is the economic factor alone that is supreme so far as the determining or moulding of the divers social relationships within a social group are concerned. Islam does not deny or under-rate the importance of the economic factor in human life, nor does it ignore the importance of a sound economic basis for the social life of a community, so as to make the moral and social virtues flourish. But it does not at all contribute towards the notion that life is but economics. It also does not believe that if economic problems are solved all the other problems of the society will also be solved as a result thereof. To make this point clearer let us, however, consider some particular cases from life. Supposing there are two young men of a similar economic status, the one being inclined to voluptuousness and engrossed in his animal passions and completely enslaved by them, whereas the other enjoys a reasonable portion of material prosperity and spends most of his extra energy in broadening his mental or spiritual horizon by acquiring some knowlege or skill. Can these two young men be treated as equals and their cases considered as identical ? Do the two represent an equal degree of virtue, goodness and success in their respective modes of living ?

We may as well take the case of a man with a strong personality to whom the people listen with deference and are ready to act upon his advice readily and still another good-for-nothing fellow, who has no personality but is just a laughter-stock among the circle of his acquaintances. Now the question is, can the solution of his economic problems help the latter in any wise ? Can he be deemed to lead a life as glorious as that of the man in the former case ?

Taking still another case we might ask if a woman endowed with grace and beauty can in any way be matched with a woman devoid of all grace and beauty ? Can the removal of economic hurdles help the ugly woman in resolving her difficulties ?

It is because of this that Islamic rationale gives basic importance not to economic values but to the non-economic ones, the moral values in particular, for it believes that it is the non-economic values that form the basis of human life for the proper organisation of which at least as much exertion and enthusiasm is called for as that needed in the case of purely economical ones. It therefore stresses a perpetual relationship between God and man; for it is this very spiritual bond between man and his God which is an excellent means for the full flourish of moral values in practical life as it lifts men from the plane of their humdrum existence where they are no better than mere slaves to their material needs and subject to internecine rivalries, hatred and rancour, to a higher, far higher plane where they are free from all these base earthly passions and where they move in a world permeated with virtue, goodness and love.

From a still another stand-point Islam holds the spiritual force in human life as of primary importance, for it is a very precious possession of man on this earth besides exercising a powerful influence on his destiny as a man. If it is paid proper attention to and organised properly it might prove not less powerful as an agent shaping human society than any other including even the economic one ; it might rather prove far more effective and powerful than all the other agents of social change. The Muslims might find enough evidence in their own history to convince them of the truth of the above statement. Thus we find that the first caliph Abu Bakr stood firm in the face of the threat of apostasy in the beginning of his rule although all the Muslims including men like Omar Bin Al Khatab did not support his stand to wage a war against the defecting tribes. Still he remained firm as a rock and did not flinch. Whence did he derive his inspiration ? Was it a material power ? or the sense of economic well-being ? or was it some human power that sustained him in that ordeal ? Surely it was none of these that inspired him or backed him up at that momentous period of his life. Had he put his faith in anyone of these he would have never dared fight against such odds at so precarious a moment in the history of Islam. It was the spiritual power alone that gave Abu Bakr the will, determination and courage to stand against the rebels who were finally subdued and turned once again good Muslims as before, leaving off their hostility towards Islam or Muslims once for all. This is a very significant chapter of human history showing how the conscious spiritual energy is transformed into material and economic power such as has no parallel in history. Similar is the case with Omar Bin Abdul Aziz who with the help of his spiritual force alone swept away the politico-social injustices created by the early Ommayedes. He rectified the injustice and successfully reformed the society resuscitating the underlying social principles of Islam. It was then that the great historical and economical miracle was witnessed : there was no longer any poor or needy man to be met with in the entire Muslim society.

Islam, therefore, gives foremost importance to spiritual power, for it does not want to deprive man of the great and miraculous benefits it can bring to him although it does not at the same time sit idle nor does it refuse material means to realize its end. Islam does believe in miracles but favours not the idle awaiting for the spiritual miracles to happen. Its constant guiding principle rather is : " God restrains with Authority that which is not restrained by the Quran."

On the other hand, it is next to impossible for men to exert themselves towards the realization of their economic ends in the way communism suggests and then be able to pay any attention to the moral values or betterment of their own spiritual life, because the exaggerated importance given to the economic aspect in communism favours but a onesided development only. It may be likened to an out-growth of human heart or liver the invariable result being that such an outgrown organ of human body hampers the proper development or functioning of other parts.

We know that there are persons who feel aversion from such a philosophical comparison of Islam and communism as we have attempted above, for they believe that such theoretical discussions carry no weight ; are rather superfluous and signify nothing. To them only the practical problems have importance which as such according to them should be given all possible precedence over all abstract considerations. They think that the things will be all right and we need not bother about any abstract questions while adopting a certain system of life except its practic-ability. Thus they are at a loss to understand that Islam and communism can ever come into conflict with each other so far as practical life is concerned. They rule out all possibility of such a conflict between the two.

We do not share their contempt of the theoretical or philosophical aspect of the problem, for we believe that the two can never be viewed in isolation from each other. However, we shall point out some of the practical differences between Islam and communism for their consideration. Some of these differences may be summed up as follows :—

(1) Islam holds that the real duty of a woman is the propagation of the human race. It, therefore, does not encourage her to leave her queendom and work in factories and fields, except of course in cases of genuine need, that is to say, in case she has no male bread earner, be he her father, brother, husband or a near one. But communism makes it obligatory for woman to go out and work in factories or fields for as many hours as the men do. Even if we over-look for the time being the underlying communist philosophy which refuses to recognize any difference between the functions as well as the psychological make-up of the sexes, the communist economy by its very nature rests on the basis of effecting increase in material means of production to the farthest possible limit. Such an increase is possible only if all the members of the community should go forth and exert themselves in factories, laboratories and fields. The woman too will have to bear an equal burden along-with other members of the community and will be off her work during the period of her confinement only. The children[1] shall as a result thereof be brought up wholesale by the state in a process similar to that of mass production.

Therefore, if we embrace the communist economy an inevitable result of it will be that woman will have

---

[1] As to the problem of upbringing children, we have already discussed it in the chapter : " Islam and Woman."

to leave her home to work outside which means in other words that one of the fundamental institutions of Islam — family the bedrock on which the whole superstructure of Islamic morality and economics rests and which shows that woman's true function is within her home while man is to do the outside work, is also dealt a fatal blow. (1) If it is said that to go out and work in factories will not be necessary for woman then surely it will be a position alien to that upheld by communism, for the communists have already made their stand too clear on the point. Now so far as effecting an increase in production is concerned, we admit that it is undoubtedly genuine and of vital importance for human existence. But it does not in any way call for the adoption of communist economy, for the communists themselves borrowed the means of increasing their production from the European capitalism. (2) The establishment of an Islamic state does in no wise forbid the use of the most modern means of agricultural and industrial production for material benefit.

---

1. This however does not negate co-operation within the family as such, just as special functions performed by the members of a community do in no wise negate co-operation among them *e.g.* farmers, artisans, engineers and doctors etc. etc.

2. Russia was in the early stage of communism extremely backward industrially. So it borrowed and developed all means of material production from Europe.

(2) The communist economy rests on a full fledged dictatorship of the proletariate, which means that the state alone decides as to the functions performed by different citizens without any regard whatsoever to their respective aptitudes or likings. The state alone controls all thought, acts, associations as well as the ends to be realised by them. At this point we must also differentiate between the dictatorship of a single ruler and the dictatorship of the state (proletariate). For, in the case of a ruler it is just possible that he be of a congenial, modest character with the welfare of his country very dear to his heart and may even at times condescend to consult the representatives of the people — real or false — before deciding a matter or enacting a law. But all these possibilities are simply out of question in the case of a dictatorship of the proletariate or state, concerned as it primarily will be with the economics alone and the realization of such ends as suit it with an iron hand. That is what is signified by the very name — dictatorship of the proletariate.

To the drawbacks of communism enumerated above we may add yet another one : it has no sound basis because of which it is often seen mucking around with theory as well as practice. Thus for instance, to begin with, it advocated an outright abolition of all private ownership and claimed to bring on a par the wages of all the different workers, but was forced to abandon its stand due to the pressure of the circumstances, as it soon found it better to allow a limited amount of private ownership and a difference in the wages of workers in proportion of their enthusiasm and pains. So communism shifted its position thus turning its back on two of the most fundamental elements in the philosophy of Karl Marx and coming as much nearer to the standpoint of Islam. How can we Muslims justify ourselves in forsaking the real and only true system of life such as humanity is all the time driven back to whenever it toys with any other system ?

WHAT NEXT ?

What ought we to do for the realization of the ideal Islam sets forth before us ? Granted that Islam is the best system to be found on this earth and that as our historical, geographical as well as international position shows, Islam is our only means to regain honour, leadership and social justice in this world, but the question is whither lies the way that leads to the realization of Islamic ideology in a world hostile to it and in the presence of the dictatorial rulers in some Muslim lands who fight against it even more furiously than its enemies from abroad do ?

Yes, whither is the way ? What ought we to do ? The answer is that there is one and only one way to attain the Islamic goal as there has always been the case with all the movements springing up in human history and that in one word is : Faith.

It was this very faith that helped the early Muslims : it still remains the only force that can help their present generation. Our stand and position today as Muslims is not in the least different from that taken up by the early Muslims. They were just a handful of men but were out to fight against two of the most powerful and proud states of that time, the Roman Empire on their left and the Persian to their right. Both of these adversaries were far superior to them in men, material wealth, art of war, in military science as well as in political insight. But despite this the great miracle happened and the handful of Muslims overpowered both the Caesars as well as the Kosroes in less than half a century. They captured their vast territories stretching from the Indian ocean to the Atlantic. How did this miracle happen ?

No materialistic interpretation of history can adequately explain this great miracle. The one thing with which we can unravel its mystery is faith and faith alone. It was this very faith that made one of these early Muslims stand up saying : Is not it true that nothing intervenes between me and paradise but that I should go and kill this man (*i.e.* the unbeliever fighting against Muslims) or get killed by him ? " And then saying this he would advance towards the battle-field as light-heartedly as if he were going to embrace his bride. Or he would jump into the field saying to his adversaries : "Do you await for us but one of two most excellent things victory or martyrdom ?" That then is the way to realize our objectives as this has always been the only course before any other movement originating in history.

There are certain people who ask us, some out of sincerity and others because of their defeatist mentality as to where is the necessary weaponry, for this purpose. Weapons ? Yes, we do need weapons, but we must not overlook the fact that the first and the foremost requisite for us is not the weapons, for weapons only cannot in this respect help a nation in the least. During the last world war the Italians possessed most effective and deadly weaponry, but still it could not save them, nor could they achieve with it any glorious success. They excelled in one thing only : running away from the battle-field leaving all their weapons in the hands of their enemies. What they wanted was not weapons but faith and inspiration.

On the other hand, we find that a handful of inspired fighters whose total strength did not exceed a hundred men at the most and whose nocturnal raiding parties never included more than six or seven men in a party at a time, so perturbed the leaders of senile old empire that they preferred leaving the country to those handful of men rather than conquer them. This faithful band of warriors did not possess deadly weapons ; they did not have heavy artillery, jet-fighters or the armoured corps. They fought with ordinary revolvers, guns and rifles but they had with them a weapon far deadlier than what their enemies possessed : they possessed faith ! They had in them the spirit the early handful of Muslims had, fighting in the way of God killing the non-believers or themselves getting killed by them. That is how they succeeded against such heavy odds.

We know that the path we have chosen for ourselves is not strewn with flowers. It is rather a way that calls for sweat, blood and tears. It demands sacrifices, self-immolation, tribulations and a readiness to exert ourselves to the utmost. But there is nothing strange in this, for similar is the case with every other movement : Sacrifices are inevitable. There is no short cut to success.

But why should we not strive hard and be ready to suffer for the lofty cause before us — for honour, glory and for social justice — when the sacrifices already experienced by us because of opprobrium, obloquy, poverty, weakness and disintegration are no less great and severe than the sacrifices called for by Islam ? Millions of men from different Arab nationalities were killed in the last world war; thousands more perished by the bombardment of the allied planes ; properties were destroyed and a large number of men were made prisoners; all material resources were confiscated without any fighting against the conquerors on the part of their possessors. But still after suffering all this Mr. Churchill was not satisfied with us. He told us bluntly: "We have saved you. Now pay us the price for it."

It was only a short while ago that the western powers were so anxious to get the Arabs agree to conclude a joint defence pact with them. Their real purpose was to incorporate at least half a million Arabs in their armed forces so as to try their deadly weapons on them and thus save the white men of America and England from their deadly effects. In doing so they forcibly captured all the food production of the Arab world, exposed its people to dishonour and disgrace and when at last they no longer needed their services kicked them out.

There is of course no escaping from death, from sacrifices and tribulations. Men died even for ignominy and ingloriousness : half a million at least laid their lives in the last great war fighting for the Allies. Why should we then flinch back from laying down our lives for Islam, for glory and truth ? When there are half a million men (as many as died for the Allies!) ready to lay down their lives for Islam the results will surely be different. There shall not remain even a single insolent dictator and tyrant on this earth, there will be no Christian or heathen imperialism to strut abroad then. Doesn't that show how we can achieve our goal ? There is the way.

Some people are perturbed over the spread of communism in the modern world. But in fact there is nothing to be upset about that, for so far as Islam is concerned the world situation has not undergone any change whatsoever. The countries under communist control at present are what formed a part of Christendom before the advent of communism and were as such as hostile towards Islam and Muslims as they are today. Russia, for instance, even before the Communist Revolution used to send groups of infiltrators into the Muslim states to sow dissension and discord among the Muslims. Similar was the case with Europe. It fought crusades against the Muslim world in the past and is still engaged in that war. Nothing has changed since so far as the Muslims or Islam is concerned.

In such a situation our stand-point must also remain unchanged. We stand exactly where the early Muslims stood when they were hemmed in from right and left by two of the most powerful countries of that time.

It is heartening to note that despite all hurdles and ruthless opposition, Islamic forces are gathering strength day by day. On balance, the revival of Islam seems but inevitable. In the world of today it is destined to play as glorious a role as it did play in the first days of its history. It promises peace and tranquility to the world of today which is wholly taken up with material pleasures and gains, and is as a result thereof stricken with conflicts and disruptions. Islam strikes a balance between the matter and the spirit, and is thus the only hope for humanity to get out of the present mess. As such the world is bound sooner or later to realize the importance of Islam and adopt its principles even if it does not formally embrace it as its religion.

As to ourselves — the workers of Islam — we submit that we are fully alive to the fact that the path before us is not a bed of roses. We Muslims will have to offer sacrifices — great and many sacrifices, in order to convince the world of the intrinsic goodness and truth of Islam. But let us ever bear in mind that the only way towards that end is but that of self-immolation : *" God will certainly aid those who aid His (cause) ; — for verily God is Full of Strength, Exalted in Might, (Able to enforce His Will)*

The Holy Quran (22 : 40).